Holt German Level 3

Komm mit!®

Lesson Planner

HOLT, RINEHART AND WINSTON
Harcourt Brace & Company

Austin • New York • Orlando • Atlanta • San Francisco • Boston • Dallas • Toronto • London

Contributing Writer

Robert Didsbury

Copyright © by Holt, Rinehart and Winston

All rights reserved. No part of this publication may be reproduced or transmitted in any form or by any means, electronic or mechanical, including photocopy, recording, or any information storage and retrieval system, without permission in writing from the publisher.

Teachers using KOMM MIT! may photocopy complete pages in sufficient quantities for classroom use only and not for resale.

Cover Photo/Illustration Credits
Background pattern: Copyright ©1992 by Dover Publications, Inc.
German clock: George Winkler/HRW Photo

KOMM MIT! is a registered trademark licensed to Holt, Rinehart and Winston.

Printed in the United States of America

ISBN 0-03-053993-5

1 2 3 4 5 6 7   066   03 02 01 00 99

Contents

To the Teacher v
Standards for Foreign Language Learning vi

Lesson Plans

Sample Multi-Level Lesson Plan 1
Sample Block Scheduling Lesson Plan 5
Kapitel 1 11
Kapitel 2 16
Kapitel 3 21
Kapitel 4 26
Kapitel 5 31
Kapitel 6 36
Kapitel 7 41
Kapitel 8 46
Kapitel 9 51
Kapitel 10 56
Kapitel 11 61
Kapitel 12 66

Homework Calendar Master 71

To the Teacher

The *Lesson Planner* is designed to guide you through *Komm mit!*, suggesting a sequence of activities and material for each chapter to best suit your needs and those of your students. You will find that the *Lesson Planner* facilitates both your evaluation of the program and documentation of your classroom work.

Standards for Foreign Language Learning

At the bottom of each page of the lesson plan is a box showing the correlations of the *Pupil's Edition* and the *Annotated Teacher's Edition* to the Standards for Foreign Language Learning. In addition, the chart on page vi provides a summary of the five major goals and the standards that correspond to each goal, so that you can more easily identify the goals covered by each section of the *Lesson Planner*. For more information on the Standards for Foreign Language Learning, see the Robert LaBouve essay on pages T44 and T45 of the Level 3 *Komm mit!* Annotated Teacher's Edition.

Sample Multi-Level Lesson Plan

Many foreign language teachers are faced with the dilemma of having students of various levels mixed together in one class. This is most commonly seen with upper level students, when enrollments are too low to justify two separate classes, or when schedule conflicts prohibit students from enrolling in the appropriate class. The sample lesson plan on pages 1-4 suggests one way you might organize a class consisting of both Level 3 and Level 4 students, using Chapter 4 of *Komm mit!*, Level 3. For more information about this chapter, such as objectives, additional suggestions, resources, and correlations to the Standards for Foreign Language Learning, see the standard lesson plans for Chapter 4 on pages 26-30.

Sample Block Scheduling Lesson Plan

There are many different configurations for block scheduling and modified block scheduling. Block periods may last for 65, 80, 90, 100, 118, or 140 minutes. A course may be scheduled for every day, every other day, or two days a week. Some schools schedule a year's work in one semester (four subjects per semester, four classes of 90 minutes daily) while others spread the curriculum over two semesters. The sample lesson plan included in this *Lesson Planner* shows how to schedule Chapter 7 of *Komm mit!* for a block program that has periods of 90 minutes held every other day, with the semester divided into three 6-week periods. Allowing 2 weeks for interrupted class time due to schoolwide testing or other special events and final semester exam, six chapters of *Komm mit!* are covered in each of two 16-week semesters (including weekly assessment). This translates into seven or eight days per chapter. For objectives, additional suggestions, resources, and correlations to the Standards for Foreign Language Learning, see the lesson plan for each particular chapter.

Chapter-specific Lesson Plans

Each chapter's lesson plan consists of objectives, suggestions for core instruction, recommendations beyond the core lesson for block scheduling, additional resources in the *Komm mit!* program, and correlations to the Standards for Foreign Language Learning. Five pages of lesson plans, arranged by chapter section, are provided per chapter. The first page gives suggestions for the Location Opener, Chapter Opener, and **Los geht's!** The second page's lesson plan addresses the **Erste Stufe;** the third, **Weiter geht's!;** the fourth, the **Zweite Stufe;** and the fifth addresses **Zum Lesen, Zum Schreiben,** and **Anwendung,** which includes suggestions for using **Kann ich's wirklich?** and **Wortschatz.**

Homework Calendar Master

On page 71 you will find a Homework Calendar Master that you can copy and distribute to your class, so that you and your students can keep track of their assignments from the *Pupil's Edition, Practice and Activity Book,* and *Grammar and Vocabulary Worksheets.*

STANDARDS FOR FOREIGN LANGUAGE LEARNING

Communication Communicate in Languages Other Than English	**Standard 1.1**	Students engage in conversations, provide and obtain information, express feelings and emotions, and exchange opinions.
	Standard 1.2	Students understand and interpret written and spoken language on a variety of topics.
	Standard 1.3	Students present information, concepts, and ideas to an audience of listeners or readers on a variety of topics.
Cultures Gain Knowledge and Understanding of Other Cultures	**Standard 2.1**	Students demonstrate an understanding of the relationship between the practices and perspectives of the culture studied.
	Standard 2.2	Students demonstrate an understanding of the relationship between the products and perspectives of the culture studied.
Connections Connect with Other Disciplines and Acquire Information	**Standard 3.1**	Students reinforce and further their knowledge of other disciplines through the foreign language.
	Standard 3.2	Students acquire information and recognize the distinctive viewpoints that are only available through the foreign language and its cultures.
Comparisons Develop Insight into the Nature of Language and Culture	**Standard 4.1**	Students demonstrate understanding of the nature of language through comparisons of the language studied and their own.
	Standard 4.2	Students demonstrate understanding of the concept of culture through comparisons of the cultures studied and their own.
Communities Participate in Multilingual Communities at Home and Around the World	**Standard 5.1**	Students use the language both within and beyond the school setting.
	Standard 5.2	Students show evidence of becoming life-long learners by using the language for personal enjoyment and enrichment.

"National Standards Report" from *Standards for Foreign Language Learning: Preparing for the 21st Century*. Copyright © 1996 by **National Standards in Foreign Language Education Project**. Reprinted by permission of the publisher.

Sample Multi-Level Lesson Plan

In a multi-level classroom environment, it is important to relieve any anxiety students might have about being placed in a multi-level learning situation. Students should be reassured that it is not demeaning or a waste of time to recycle activities or to share knowledge and skills with fellow students. Third-year students need to know that they are not second-class citizens and that they can benefit from their classmates' greater experience with the language. Fourth-year students need reassurance that you will devote time to them and challenge them with different assignments. Fourth-year students should also be made aware of the benefits they will gain by helping or teaching third-year students, including increased confidence in their own language skills and the satisfaction of helping others achieve.

You can relieve your own apprehension by remembering that, after one year of classroom instruction, no class is ever truly homogeneous. Despite being made up of students with the same amount of "seat time," every class comprises multiple layers of language skills, knowledge, motivation, and ability.

Addressing these individual differences in a single-level classroom requires effort and good planning, and you will find the same to be true of a multi-level classroom. Meeting the needs of students at different levels will be made easier if you work towards the goal of making students less dependent on you for the successful completion of their activities, by placing more responsibility for learning on the students, and by implementing creative individual, pair, and group activities.

Pair and group activities are very effective in multi-level classrooms and can accomplish a variety of objectives, depending on how you group your students. For example, pairing a fourth-year student with a third-year student would create a peer-tutoring situation, and grouping several fourth- and third-year students together could foster a cross-level attitude of cooperation and teamwork. There will be other times when you will want to group students by level, for example, when providing students with material that is appropriate for their level, but which would be either too basic or too advanced for students at a different level. The decision to have students work in pairs or groups, multi-level or same level, should be tied to your goals for that day. You may find it effective to have students take part in the decision as to what type of group works best for them.

Chapter 4 Verhältnis zu anderen

BEGINNING THE CHAPTER (pp. 80–81)

(All references in this lesson plan are to *Komm mit!*, Level 3.)

Objectives: To preview the functional expressions and vocabulary that will be covered in this chapter.

BOTH LEVELS TOGETHER
- See Focusing on Outcomes and Motivating Activity, p.79I.

LOS GEHT'S! (pp. 82–83)

BOTH LEVELS TOGETHER
- See Motivating Activity, p. 79J.

LEVEL 3 STUDENTS
- Have students copy the chart in Activity 1, p. 83, and add a third column labeled **Anderen**. Play the audio recording of **Verhältnis zu Eltern und Freunden** *(Audio CD 4)*. Allow students time to complete their chart.

LEVEL 4 STUDENTS
- Have students read **Verhältnis zu Eltern und Freunden**. Then have them compose and write their own answers to the questions.

BOTH LEVELS TOGETHER
- Go over the charts the Level 3 students completed. Then have the Level 4 students give their answers to the questions as the others listen.

LEVEL 3 STUDENTS
- Create four groups and assign the role of one of the four German students to each group. Replay the recording of **Verhältnis zu Eltern und Freunden**, pp. 82–83, and have group members try to supply the answers given by their assigned character.

LEVEL 4 STUDENTS
- See Closure, p. 79J.
- Have students do Activities 1 and 2, *Practice and Activity Book*, p. 40.

ERSTE STUFE (pp. 84–87)

Objectives: Students will learn to express agreement.

BOTH LEVELS TOGETHER
- See the related Teaching Suggestion, p. 79K.

LEVEL 3 STUDENTS
- Present **Wortschatz**, p. 84. See Presentation, p. 79K.
- Have students do Activity 1, *Grammar and Vocabulary Worksheets*, p. 28.

LEVEL 4 STUDENTS
- Have students write a paragraph or a dialogue in

Komm mit! Level 3, Sample Multi-Level Lesson Plan

which they incorporate as much of the new vocabulary as possible from **Wortschatz**, p. 84.

BOTH LEVELS TOGETHER
- Have Level 4 students read the paragraphs they wrote for **Wortschatz**, p. 84.

LEVEL 3 STUDENTS
- Have students write Activity 4, p. 84.
- Have students do Communicative Activity 4-1, *Activities for Communication,* pp. 13–14.

LEVEL 4 STUDENTS
- Distribute copies of *Teaching Transparency 4-1, Teaching Transparencies.* Have groups prepare family counseling sessions for each picture.

BOTH LEVELS TOGETHER
- Play the audio recording for Activity 5, p. 85 *(Audio CD 4),* and check for comprehension.
- Have Level 3 students pair off with Level 4 students to do Activity 6, p. 85.
- Present **So sagt man das!** *(Agreeing),* p. 85. See Presentation, p. 79K.
- Play the audio recording for Activity 7, p. 85 *(Audio CD 4),* and check for comprehension.

LEVEL 3 STUDENTS
- Have students do Communicative Activity 4-2, *Activities for Communication,* pp. 15–16.

LEVEL 4 STUDENTS
- Have students do Activity 8, p. 85.

BOTH LEVELS TOGETHER
- Have Level 4 students discuss their answers to Activity 8, p. 85. Level 3 students should say whether they agree or disagree.
- Present **Ein wenig Landeskunde,** p. 86. See Presentation, p. 79L.

LEVEL 4 STUDENTS
- Have students write about the cliques at their school and how they feel about cliques.

LEVEL 3 STUDENTS
- Present **Ein wenig Grammatik** *(Ordinal numbers),* p. 86. See Presentation, p. 79K.
- Have students do Activity 9, p. 86.
- Have students do Activity 3, *Grammar and Vocabulary Worksheets,* p. 29.

BOTH LEVELS TOGETHER
- Have students read the chart entitled **Mit wem verbringen Jugendliche ihre Freizeit?** Take a similar survey of the class.
- Have students do Activity 4, *Practice and Activity Book,* p. 42.

LEVEL 3 STUDENTS
- Have students write Activity 10, p. 86, in class or for homework.

LEVEL 4 STUDENTS
- Have students do Activity 8, *Practice and Activity Book,* p. 44.

BOTH LEVELS TOGETHER
- Present **Grammatik** *(Relative clauses),* p. 87. See Presentation, p. 79L.

LEVEL 3 STUDENTS
- Have students write Activity 11, p. 87.
- Have students do Activities 4 and 5, *Grammar and Vocabulary Worksheets,* pp. 30–31.

LEVEL 4 STUDENTS
- Distribute a copy of the paragraph in Activity 11, p. 87, with the relative clauses deleted. Have students rewrite the paragraph, adding relative clauses that reflect their own situation.

BOTH LEVELS TOGETHER
- Show the video clip **Im Freizeitzentrum**, *Video Program (Videocassette 1).*

LEVEL 3 STUDENTS
- Have students do Activity Master 1, *Video Guide,* p. 19.

LEVEL 4 STUDENTS
- Have students work in groups to do the Post-viewing Activity, *Video Guide,* p. 18.

LEVEL 3 STUDENTS
- Have students take Quiz 4-1A or 4-1B, *Testing Program,* pp. 67–70.
- Have students do Situation 4-1: Role-playing, *Activities for Communication,* p. 120.

LEVEL 4 STUDENTS
- Have students do Performance Assessment, p. 79M.

WEITER GEHT'S! (pp. 88–89)

BOTH LEVELS TOGETHER
- Do Motivating Activity, p. 79M.

LEVEL 4 STUDENTS
- Ask students to reread **Verhältnis zu Eltern und Freunden,** pp. 82–83. Have them predict what the attitude of these four students would be toward fringe groups at school and tell the Level 3 students their predictions.

BOTH LEVELS TOGETHER
- Play the first half of the audio recording of **Verhältnis zu anderen Leuten** *(Audio CD 4).* Tell students to listen for the gist of each speaker's remarks. Discuss their findings and whether or not the predictions of the Level 4 students were accurate.

LEVEL 4 STUDENTS
- Have students predict what the attitude of these same four Germans would be toward foreigners and tell Level 3 students their predictions.

BOTH LEVELS TOGETHER
- Play the second half of the audio recording of **Verhältnis zu anderen Leuten** *(Audio CD 4)*. Tell students to determine the attitude of each speaker toward foreign students. Discuss whether or not the predictions of the Level 4 students were accurate.

LEVEL 3 STUDENTS
- Have students do Activity 12 and #1 and #2 of Activity 13, p. 89.

LEVEL 4 STUDENTS
- Have students work in small groups to reread the conversation, changing it as they read to refer to their own school population.

BOTH LEVELS TOGETHER
- Have the Level 4 students present to the Level 3 students their revised version of the conversation in **Verhältnis zu anderen Leuten.**
- Have students discuss #3 of Activity 13, p. 89.

ZWEITE STUFE (pp. 90–94)

Objectives: Students will learn to give advice, introduce another point of view, and hypothesize.

BOTH LEVELS TOGETHER
- See the related Teaching Suggestion, p. 79N.

LEVEL 3 STUDENTS
- Present **Wortschatz**, p. 90. See Presentation, p. 79N.
- Have students do Activity 6, *Grammar and Vocabulary Worksheets*, p. 32.

LEVEL 4 STUDENTS
- Ask students to write the sentences in **Wortschatz**, p. 90, and then add another that continues the thought of the first.

BOTH LEVELS TOGETHER
- Play the recording for Activity 14, p. 90 *(Audio CD 4)*, and check for comprehension.

LEVEL 4 STUDENTS
- Have students read the letters in Realia 4-1, *Activities for Communication*, p. 66. Then have them do suggestion 5, p. 69.

BOTH LEVELS TOGETHER
- Have students work in mixed-level groups to do Activity 15, p. 90.
- Present **So sagt man das!** *(Giving advice; introducing another point of view)*, p. 91.

LEVEL 3 STUDENTS
- Have students do Activity 7, *Grammar and Vocabulary Worksheets*, p. 33.

LEVEL 4 STUDENTS
- Have students do Activities 4 and 8, *Practice and Activity Book*, pp. 47, 49.

BOTH LEVELS TOGETHER
- Play the recording for Activity 16, p. 91 *(Audio CD 4)*, and check for comprehension.

LEVEL 4 STUDENTS
- See For Individual Needs: Challenge, p. 79N, related to Activity 16, p. 91.

BOTH LEVELS TOGETHER
- Have students pair off by level to do Activity 17, p. 91.
- Present **So sagt man das!** *(Hypothesizing)* and **Ein wenig Grammatik** *(Using hätte and wäre in place of würde haben and würde sein)*, p. 92. See Presentations, p. 79O.

LEVEL 3 STUDENTS
- Have students do Activity 8, *Grammar and Vocabulary Worksheets*, p. 34.
- Have students do Activity 2, *Practice and Activity Book*, p. 46.

LEVEL 4 STUDENTS
- Distribute copies of *Teaching Transparency 4-2, Teaching Transparencies*. Have students tell a partner what they would do if they were the person featured in each picture.

BOTH LEVELS TOGETHER
- Show *Teaching Transparency 4-2, Teaching Transparencies*. Have Level 4 students tell the others what they would do in each situation pictured. Level 3 students might say that they would do the same or might suggest taking another course of action.
- Play the recording for Activity 19, p. 92 *(Audio CD 4)*, and check for comprehension.

LEVEL 3 STUDENTS
- Distribute copies of a map of the western United States. As students listen to the recording for Activity 19, p. 92, have them trace on the map the itineraries the speakers suggest.

LEVEL 4 STUDENTS
- Distribute copies of the recording script for Activity 19, p. 92, and have students rewrite the conversation as if the girls were planning a trip to the students' area.

BOTH LEVELS TOGETHER
- Have students do Activities 20 and 21, p. 92.
- Present **Grammatik**, *(The genitive case)*, p. 93. See Presentation, p. 79O.

LEVEL 3 STUDENTS
- Have students write Activities 22 and 23, p. 93.
- Have students do Activities 9–11, *Grammar and Vocabulary Worksheets*, pp. 35–36.
- Have students do Activities 3 and 5, *Practice and Activity Book*, pp. 47, 48.

LEVEL 4 STUDENTS
- Have students take the self-test in Realia 4-3, *Activities for Communication*, p. 68.

BOTH LEVELS TOGETHER
- Present **Landeskunde,** p. 94.

LEVEL 3 STUDENTS
- Have students do Activities A and B, p. 94.

LEVEL 4 STUDENTS
- Have students do Activities 1–3, *Practice and Activity Book,* p. 50.

LEVEL 3 STUDENTS
- Have students take Quiz 4-2A or 4-2B, *Testing Program,* pp. 71–74.

LEVEL 4 STUDENTS
- Have students do Performance Assessment, p. 79Q.

ZUM SCHREIBEN (p. 95)

Objectives: Students will learn to determine the purpose of their writing.

BOTH LEVELS TOGETHER
- Do Motivating Activity, p. 79Q, and read and discuss **Schreibtip,** p. 95.
- Have students do Activities A–C, p. 95. See the related suggestions, pp. 79Q–79R.

ZUM LESEN (pp. 96–99)

Objectives: Students will learn to determine the main idea of a story.

BOTH LEVELS TOGETHER
- Do Motivating Activity, p. 79R, and read and discuss **Lesetrick,** p. 96.
- Have students form multi-level groups and read **Ein Tisch ist ein Tisch.**
- Have these multi-level groups do Activities 1–10, pp. 96–99.

LEVEL 3 STUDENTS
- Have students do Activities 11 and 12, p. 99.

LEVEL 4 STUDENTS
- Have students do the activity suggested in Closure, p. 79S.

ANWENDUNG (pp. 100–101)

Objectives: Students will review and integrate all four skills and culture in preparation for Chapter 4 assessment.

BOTH LEVELS TOGETHER
- Play the recording for Activity 1, p. 100 *(Audio CD 4),* and check for comprehension.
- Have students form multi-level groups to do Activities 2 and 5, pp. 100, 101.
- Have students do Activities 3 and 4, pp. 100–101.

LEVEL 3 STUDENTS
- Have students pair off to do Activity 6, p. 101.

LEVEL 4 STUDENTS
- Have students do Activity 9, *Practice and Activity Book,* p. 49.

KANN ICH'S WIRKLICH? (p. 102)

Objectives: Students will evaluate their understanding of the functions, vocabulary, grammar, and culture presented in Chapter 4.

BOTH LEVELS TOGETHER
- Have students work in multi-level groups to do Activities 1–4, p. 102.

ASSESSMENT

LEVEL 3 STUDENTS
- Have students take the Chapter Test, *Testing Program,* pp. 75–80.

LEVEL 4 STUDENTS
- Have students do Activity 9, *Practice and Activity Book,* p. 49.

Sample Block Scheduling Lesson Plan

There are many different configurations for block scheduling and modified block scheduling. Block periods may last for 65, 80, 90, 100, 118, or 140 minutes. A course may be scheduled for every day, every other day, or two days a week. Some schools schedule a year's work in one semester (four subjects per semester, four classes of 90 minutes daily) while others spread the curriculum over two semesters. The following sample lesson plan shows how to schedule Chapter 7 of *Komm mit!* for a block program that has periods of 90 minutes held every other day, with the semester divided into three six-week periods. Allowing two weeks for interrupted class time due to schoolwide testing or other special events and a final semester exam, six chapters of *Komm mit!* are covered in each of two sixteen-week semesters (including weekly assessment). This translates into seven to eight days per chapter. For objectives, additional suggestions, resources, and correlations to the Standards for Foreign Language Learning, see the lesson plan for each particular chapter.

Kapitel 7 Ohne Reklame geht es nicht!

DAY ONE

LOCATION OPENER (pp. 151A–155)
Objectives: Students will learn about famous people, historical events, and places in Frankfurt.
- See the Pre-viewing Suggestions, *Video Guide*, p. 29.
- Have students do the Pre-viewing Activity, *Video Guide*, p. 30.
- Show **Komm mit nach Frankfurt!**, *Video Program (Videocassette 2)*. See the Viewing Suggestions, *Video Guide*, p. 29.
- Have students do the Viewing Activity, *Video Guide*, p. 30.
- See the Post-viewing Suggestions, *Video Guide*, p. 29.

CHAPTER OPENER (pp. 156–157)
Objectives: Students will discuss the chapter theme and identify the learning outcomes for Chapter 7.
- Go over the results of the Chapter 6 Test with students.
- Do Motivating Activity, p. 155I.
- Have students preview the learning outcomes listed on p. 157. See Focusing on Outcomes, p. 155I.

LOS GEHT'S! – Werbung—ja oder nein? (pp. 158–159)
Objectives: Students will listen to German teenagers respond to an opinion poll about advertising.
- Do Motivating Activity, p. 155J.
- Before presenting **Werbung—ja oder nein?**, pp. 158–159, you might choose to present from **Wortschatz,** p. 160, the new vocabulary that students will encounter in **Los geht's!** See Presentation, p. 155K.
- Play the audio recording of **Werbung—ja oder nein?** *(Audio CD 7)*.
- Replay the audio recording of Stefan's description of the frozen food commercial. Ask students if they can recall any American commercials that also present an unrealistic picture of **gemütlich** family life.
- Have students do Activity 1, p. 159.
- Have students do Activity 2, p. 159. See Thinking Critically: Analyzing and the related Teaching Suggestion, p. 155J.

HOMEWORK
- Have students do Activities 1 and 2, *Practice and Activity Book,* p. 79.

DAY TWO

LOS GEHT'S! (pp. 158–159)
- Check homework, Activities 1 and 2, *Practice and Activity Book,* p. 79.

ERSTE STUFE (pp. 160–164)
Objectives: Students will learn to express annoyance and to compare.
- Have students quickly read **Werbung—pro und contra,** p. 160, to get the gist of the comments. Ask them which comments they think are favorable to commercials and which are unfavorable. Then have students reread **Werbung—pro und contra.**
- Have students do Communicative Activity 7-1 or 7-2, *Activities for Communication,* pp. 25–26.
- Present **Wortschatz,** p. 160. See Presentation, p. 155K.
- Have students do Activities 1–3, *Grammar and Vocabulary Worksheets,* pp. 55–56.
- Present **So sagt man das!** *(Expressing annoyance),* p. 161. See Presentation, p. 155L.
- Play the audio recording for Activity 3, p. 161 *(Audio CD 7)*.
- Have students do Activity 4, *Grammar and Vocabulary Worksheets,* p. 57.
- Have students work in groups to do Activities 4 and 5, p. 161.
- Present **So sagt man das!** *(Comparing),* p. 161. See Presentation, p. 155L.
- Play the audio recording for Activity 6, p. 161 *(Audio CD 7)*, and check for comprehension. See For Additional Practice, p. 155L.
- Have students do Activity 5, *Grammar and Vocabulary Worksheets,* p. 57.
- Present **Grammatik** *(derselbe, der gleiche),* p. 162. See Presentation, p. 155L.
- Have students do Activities 6 and 7, *Grammar and Vocabulary Worksheets,* p. 58.
- Have students pair off to do Activity 7, p. 162.
- Have students work in groups to do Activity 8, p. 162.

Komm mit! Level 3, Sample Block Scheduling Lesson Plan

Copyright © by Holt, Rinehart and Winston. All rights reserved.

- See Reteaching: **Derselbe** and **der gleiche**, p. 155M.

HOMEWORK
- Have students do Activities 1–3, *Practice and Activity Book,* pp. 80–81.

DAY THREE

ERSTE STUFE (pp. 160–164)
- Check homework: Activities 1–3, *Practice and Activity Book,* pp. 80–81.
- Show the video clip **Ein großes Angebot**, *Video Program (Videocassette 2).* See Teaching Suggestions, *Video Guide,* p. 32, and Activity Master 1, *Video Guide,* p. 33.
- Present **Grammatik** *(Adjective endings following determiners of quantity),* p. 163. See Presentation, p. 155M.
- Have students do Activity 8, *Grammar and Vocabulary Worksheets,* p. 59.
- Have students do Activity 4, *Practice and Activity Book,* p. 81.
- Have students pair off to do Activity 9, p. 163.
- Play the audio recording for Activity 10, p. 163 *(Audio CD 7),* and check for comprehension.
- Have students work in groups to do Activity 11, p. 163. Before they begin, have them familiarize themselves with the adjectives and then rank the words in descending order from the most to the least forceful.
- Show *Teaching Transparency 7-1, Teaching Transparencies,* for further practice composing slogans and ads.
- Have students pair off to do Activities 12 and 13, p. 164.
- For further practice analyzing advertisements, use Realia 7-2 and 7-3, *Activities for Communication,* pp. 82–83.
- Have students work in groups to do Activity 14, p. 164. See Group Work, p. 155M.

HOMEWORK
- Have students write Activity 15, p. 164, in their journal.
- Tell students to study for Quiz 7-1A or 7-1B on the **Erste Stufe.**

DAY FOUR

ERSTE STUFE (pp. 87–91)
- Check homework (Activity 15, p. 164) by viewing students' journals and asking for volunteers to read one of their entries.
- Give Quiz 7-1A or 7-1B on the **Erste Stufe**, *Testing Program,* pp. 147–150.

LANDESKUNDE (p. 165)
Objectives: Students will read about an American exchange student's experience with commercial interruptions on German television.
- Present **Landeskunde,** p. 165. See the related Teacher Note, p. 155M.
- Have students do Activities 1 and 2, *Practice and Activity Book,* p. 84.

WEITER GEHT'S (pp. 166–167)
Objectives: Students will listen to German students and their teacher discuss a particular TV advertisement.
- Do Motivating Activity, p. 155O.
- Before presenting **Image-Werbung**, pp. 166–167, you might choose to present **Wortschatz**, p. 168, which contains the new vocabulary that students will encounter in **Weiter geht's!** See Presentation, p. 155P.
- Have students listen with their books closed as you play the audio recording *(Audio CD 7)* of the description of the commercial for the chocolate drink on p. 166.
- Have students open their books and read the description of the commercial for the chocolate drink on p. 166. See Thinking Critically: Drawing Inferences, p. 155O.
- Have students do questions 1 and 2 of Activity 16, p. 167.
- Continue playing the audio recording of **Image-Werbung** *(Audio CD 7),* in which the class discusses commercials with the teacher. Pause after the teacher's first remark at the top of p. 167. Ask students if they agree with the German students on the role of children in commercials.
- Have students listen to the remainder of the audio recording of **Image**-Werbung. Tell them to listen carefully for the criticisms the German students have of commercials.
- Have students do questions 3 and 4 of Activity 16, p. 167.
- Have students read the ad on p. 167 and identify the sponsor and the product(s) advertised. Call attention to the column pictured on p. 167. Ask what columns such as this are called (**Litfaßsäulen**) and what their purpose is. See Culture Notes, p. 155I.
- Replay the segment of the audio recording of **Image**-Werbung in which the classmates talk about their own experiences with the chocolate drink. Ask students if they have had a common experience with such a product in their childhood.
- Have students write a description of their favorite commercial, patterned after the chocolate drink ad on p. 166.

HOMEWORK
- Have students do Activity 1, *Practice and Activity Book,* p.85.

DAY FIVE

WEITER GEHT'S (pp. 166–167)
- Check homework: Activity 1, *Practice and Activity Book,* p.85.

ZWEITE STUFE (pp. 168–171)
Objectives: Students will learn to elicit agreement and

agree and to express conviction, uncertainty, and what seems to be true.
- See the related Teaching Suggestion, p. 155P.
- Present **Wortschatz,** p. 168. See Presentation, p. 155P.
- Have students do Activities 9 and 10, *Grammar and Vocabulary Worksheets,* p. 60.
- Have students do Communicative Activity 7-3, *Activities for Communication,* pp. 27–28.
- Present **So sagt man das!** *(Eliciting agreement and agreeing),* p. 168. See Presentation, p. 155P.
- Have students do Activity 11, *Grammar and Vocabulary Worksheets,* p. 61.
- Play the audio recording for Activity 17, p. 168 *(Audio CD 7)* three times. The first time, ask students to note the ads that the editors are considering. The second time, have students note the reactions to the ads. The third time, have students note the ad upon which the editors finally agree.
- Have students pair off to do Activity 18, p. 169.
- Have students do Communicative Activity 7-4, *Activities for Communication,* pp. 27–28.
- Present **Ein wenig Grammatik** *(Review of relative clauses with forms of der, die, das)* and **Grammatik** *(Introducing relative clauses with **was** and **wo**),* p. 169. See Presentation, p. 155P.
- Have students do Activities 12 and 13, *Grammar and Vocabulary Worksheets,* p. 62.
- Have students pair off to do Activities 19 and 20, p. 170.
- Present **So sagt man das!** *(Expressing conviction, uncertainty, and what seems to be true),* p. 170. See Presentation, p. 155P.
- Have students do Activity 6, *Practice and Activity Book,* p. 88.
- Play the audio recording for Activity 22, p. 170 *(Audio CD 7).* Have students reread beforehand the description of the commercial for **Schoko-Sam,** p. 166, which is the subject of the recording.
- Present **Grammatik** *(irgendein and irgendwelche),* p. 171. See Presentation, p. 155P.
- Have students do Activity 23, p. 171, and Activity 14, *Grammar and Vocabulary Worksheets,* p. 63.
- Present **Wortschatz,** p. 171. See Presentation, p. 155Q.
- Have students do Activity 15, *Grammar and Vocabulary Worksheets,* p. 63.
- Have students pair off to do Activity 24, p. 171. See For Individual Needs: Challenge, p. 155Q.
- Have students work in groups to do Activity 25, p. 171.

HOMEWORK
- Have students write Activity 26, p. 171, in their journal.
- Tell students to study for Quiz 7-2A or 7-2B on the **Zweite Stufe.**

DAY SIX

ZWEITE STUFE (pp. 168–171)
- Check homework: Activity 26, p. 171.
- Give Quiz 7-2A or 7-2B on the **Zweite Stufe,** *Testing Program,* pp. 151–154.

ZUM LESEN (pp. 171–174)
Objectives: Students will learn to use pictures and print type as clues to meaning.
- Do Motivating Activity, p. 155R.
- Read and discuss **Lesetrick,** p. 172.
- Have students do Activities 1 and 2, pp. 172–173. See Teaching Suggestions, p. 155R.
- Have students do Activities 3–9, pp. 173–174. See the Teacher Note for Activity 4, p. 155R.
- Have students do Activity 10, p. 174. See the related Teacher Note, p. 155R.
- See Closure, p. 155R.

ZUM SCHREIBEN (p. 175)
Objectives: Students will learn to use tone and word choice for effect.
- Do Motivating Activity, p. 155S.
- Discuss the writing strategy presented in **Schreibtip,** p. 175.
- Have students complete Activity A (**Vorbereiten**), p. 175. See the second Teacher Note, the first Teaching Suggestion, and For Individual Needs: Challenge, p. 155S.
- Have students complete Activity B (**Ausführen**), p. 175. See first Teacher Note and the second Teaching Suggestion for Writing, p.155S.
- Have students complete Activity C (**Überarbeiten**), p. 175.
- As a follow-up activity, have students exchange their letters and write a response from the makers of the product that attempts to placate the complaining consumer.

HOMEWORK
- Have students do Activities 1–7, *Practice and Activity Book,* pp. 90–91.

DAY SEVEN

ZUM LESEN (pp. 171–174)
- Check homework: Activities 1–7, *Practice and Activity Book,* pp. 90–91.

ANWENDUNG (pp. 176–177)
Objectives: Students will review the functions, vocabulary, grammar, and culture in preparation for the Chapter Test.
- Have students read **Im kreativen Rausch,** p. 176, and do Activity 1.
- Play the audio recording for Activity 2, p. 177 *(Audio CD 7),* and check for comprehension. See the related Teaching Suggestion, p. 155T.
- Have students work in groups to do Activity 3, p. 177. Refer them to the opinions stated in Activity

---

Komm mit! Level 3, Sample Block Scheduling Lesson Plan

Copyright © by Holt, Rinehart and Winston. All rights reserved.

18, p. 169, and Activity 25, p. 171.
- Have students work in groups to do Activity 4, p. 177. See Cooperative Learning, p. 155T.
- Have students write Activity 5, p. 177.
- Show **Videoclips: Werbung,** *Video Program (Videocassette 2).* See Teaching Suggestions, *Video Guide,* p. 32, and Activity Masters 1 and 2, *Video Guide,* pp. 33–34.
- Have students work in groups to do Activity 6, p. 177.

KANN ICH'S WIRKLICH?/WORTSCHATZ (pp. 178–179)
Objectives: Students will evaluate their understanding of the functions, vocabulary, and grammar presented in Chapter 7.
- Have students do Activities 1–6, p. 178, individually or with a partner.
- Have students review the vocabulary in the **Wortschatz,** p. 179. See Teaching Suggestion and Game, p. 155T.

HOMEWORK
- Tell students to study for the Chapter Test.

DAY EIGHT

CHAPTER TEST
- Give the Chapter Test for Chapter 7, *Testing Program,* pp. 155–160.
- Administer the Speaking Test for Chapter 7, *Testing Program,* p. 298.

Chapter Lesson Plans

Teacher's Name _____ Class _____ Date _____

Das Land am Meer (Wiederholungskapitel)

Beginning the chapter (pp. T68–7)

Activities in the shaded boxes enhance the basic lesson and are ideal for **block scheduling**.

Lesson Plans

Location Opener

Objectives
Students will learn about famous people, historical events, and places in the **neue Bundesländer**.

- Have students do the Pre-viewing Activity, *Video Guide*, p. 2.
- Show **Komm mit in die neuen Bundesländer!**, *Video Program (Videocassette 1)*.
- Have students do the Viewing Activity, *Video Guide*, p. 2.
- See the Post-viewing Suggestions, *Video Guide*, p. 1.
- Play some of the music of Bach and have students read some of Goethe's poems.

Chapter Opener

- Do Motivating Activity, p. 3I.
- Have students look at photo #1, p. 4. Identify the boys by name: Gregor (wearing the cap) and Johannes. See Teaching Suggestion, p. 3I.
- Ask students to tell you whatever they can about photo #1. They might tell who the people are, where they are, what they are wearing, and what they are doing.
- Have students look at photo #2, p. 5. See the related Teaching Suggestion, p. 3I.
- Ask students what Gregor might say in reaction to Johannes' complaint in the caption of photo #2.
- Have students look at photo #3, p. 5. See Thinking Critically: Drawing Inferences, p. 3I.
- Ask students who they think is asking the question in the caption of photo #3 and how the other boy might answer.
- See Focusing on Outcomes, p. 3I.

Los geht's!

Objectives
Students will listen to a conversation between Johannes and Gregor, meeting for the first time after summer vacation.

- Have students do Activities 1–3, p. 7. See the related suggestions, p. 3K.
- Have students do Activity 1, *Practice and Activity Book,* p. 1.
- Do Motivating Activity, p. 3J.
- Play the audio recording of **Zwei Freunde treffen sich** *(Audio CD 1)*. See Teaching Suggestion, p. 3J.
- Have students answer the questions in Activity 1, p. 7.
- Have students read **Zwei Freunde treffen sich** and do Activities 2 and 3, p. 7.
- Have students do Activities 1 and 2, *Practice and Activity Book,* p. 1.
- See Closure, p. 3J.

Resources
For correlated print and audiovisual materials, see *Annotated Teacher's Edition*, pp. 3A–3B.

STANDARDS FOR FOREIGN LANGUAGE LEARNING
Location Opener *Pupil's Edition:* (3.1; 4.2) *Annotated Teacher's Edition:* (3.1; 5.2)
Chapter Opener *Pupil's Edition:* (4.1; 4.2) *Annotated Teacher's Edition:* (1.1)
Los geht's! *Pupil's Edition:* (1.2) *Annotated Teacher's Edition:* (2.2; 4.2)

Komm mit! Level 3   Lesson Planner **11**
Copyright © by Holt, Rinehart and Winston. All rights reserved.

Teacher's Name _____ Class _____ Date _____

KAPITEL 1

Das Land am Meer (Wiederholungskapitel)

Erste Stufe (pp. 8–12)

Activities in the shaded boxes enhance the basic lesson and are ideal for **block scheduling**.

Lesson Plans

Objectives
Students will review reporting past events, asking how someone liked something, expressing enthusiasm or disappointment, and responding enthusiastically or sympathetically.

Motivate
See Teaching Suggestion, p. 3K.

Teach
1. Have students read **Rügen,** p. 8, and answer the questions in Activity 4, p. 8.
2. Present **Ein wenig Grammatik** *(Prepositions followed by the dative case)*, p. 9. See Presentation, p. 3K.
3. Present **Wortschatz,** p. 9.
   Have students do Activities 1-4, *Grammar and Vocabulary Worksheets,* pp. 1–2.
4. Present **So sagt man das!** *(Reporting past events)*, p. 9. See Presentation, p. 3K.
5. Play the audio recording for Activity 5, p. 9 *(Audio CD 1)*, and check for comprehension.
6. Have students pair off to do Activities 6 and 7, p. 9.
7. Present **Ein wenig Grammatik** *(The conversational past)*, p. 10.
8. Have students pair off to do Activities 8 and 9, p. 10.
9. Present **Wortschatz,** p. 10. See Presentation, p. 3L.
10. Play the audio recording for Activity 10, p. 10 *(Audio CD 1)*, and check for comprehension.
11. Have students work in groups to do Activity 11, p. 11.
    Have students do Activities 5 and 6, *Grammar and Vocabulary Worksheets,* p. 3.
12. Have students pair off to do Activities 12 and 13, p. 11.
13. Present **So sagt man das!** *(Asking how someone liked something; expressing enthusiasm . . .*, p. 12.
    Have students do Activity 5, *Practice and Activity Book,* p. 4.
14. Play the audio recording for Activity 14, p. 12 *(Audio CD 1)*, and check for comprehension.
15. Present **Ein wenig Grammatik** *(Verbs always used with the dative case)*, p. 12. See Presentation, p. 3M.
16. Have students write Activity 16, p. 12, in class or for homework. See Teacher Note, p. 3M.

Additional Practice Options for Erste Stufe
- *Grammar and Vocabulary Worksheets,* pp. 1–4
- *Practice and Activity Book,* pp. 2–5
- Communicative Activities 1-1 and 1-2, *Activities for Communication,* pp. 1–2
- Situation 1-1 Interview and Role-playing, *Activities for Communication,* pp. 113–114
- Additional Listening Activities 1-1, 1-2, and 1-3, *Listening Activities,* pp. 7–8 *(Audio CD 1)*
- Realia 1-1, *Activities for Communication,* p. 51
- Teaching Transparency 1-1, *Teaching Transparencies*
- Additional Grammar Practice, *Pupil's Edition,* Activities 1-3, pp. R40–R41

Close
Close, p. 3M.

Assess
Quiz 1-1A or 1-1B, *Testing Program,* pp. 1–4, and/or Performance Assessment, p. 3M

Resources
For correlated print and audiovisual materials, see *Annotated Teacher's Edition,* pp. 3A–3B.

STANDARDS FOR FOREIGN LANGUAGE LEARNING
Erste Stufe *Pupil's Edition:* (1.1; 1.3; 4.1) *Annotated Teacher's Edition:* (1.2)

12 Lesson Planner

Komm mit! Level 3

Teacher's Name _____ Class _____ Date _____

Das Land am Meer (Wiederholungskapitel)

Weiter geht's! (pp. 14–15)

Activities in the shaded boxes enhance the basic lesson and are ideal for **block scheduling**.

Lesson Plans

Weiter geht's!

Objectives
Students will listen as Gregor stops by to visit Johannes and his family.

- Do Motivating Activity, p. 30, in which students talk about visiting a friend's home.
- Divide the class into two groups. Play the audio recording of **Gregor besucht Johannes** (Audio CD 1) and have students listen with their books closed. Tell one group to note the foods that Johannes and Gregor mention. Have the other group note where Johannes spent his vacation, what the weather was like, and what happened to him.
- For a slower pace, distribute a list of foods which includes those mentioned by Johannes and Gregor. Play the audio recording of **Gregor besucht Johannes** (Audio CD 1) and have students listen with their books closed. They should circle on the list those foods that they hear mentioned. They might also put a plus or a minus sign next to each to indicate whether the person who mentions the food likes or dislikes it.
- Have students read to themselves the questions in Activity 17, p. 15.
- Play the audio recording of **Gregor besucht Johannes** (Audio CD 1) as students read along in their books.
- Have students answer the questions in Activity 17, p. 15. See For Individual Needs: Challenge, p. 30.
- Have students pair off to write speech bubbles for each of the photos on pp. 14 and 15. They should find lines in **Gregor besucht Johannes** that the boys might be saying in each photo. Then have partners read their dialogues aloud.
- Have students read Gregor besucht Johannes again and do Activity 18, p. 15.
- To extend Activity 18, p. 15, ask students to find all of Johannes' and Gregor's remarks in which they express or ask about their likes and dislikes. Ask them to rephrase the remarks without using **mögen**.
- To review expressions for inquiring about someone's health and responding, and the vocabulary for ailments, show Teaching Transparency 6-1, Level 2 *Teaching Transparencies*, which pictures teenagers with different ailments.
- To review expressions for asking about and expressing pain and the vocabulary for physical injuries, show Teaching Transparency 6-2, Level 2 *Teaching Transparencies*, which pictures people with various injuries in a doctor's waiting room.
- Have students do Activity 19, p. 15.
- For further challenge, replay the audio recording of **Gregor besucht Johannes.** Pause the recording from time to time and ask students if they can come up with the next line, or an approximation thereof.
- See Closure, p. 30.
- Have students do Activity 1, *Practice and Activity Book*, p. 6.

Resources
For correlated print and audiovisual materials, see *Annotated Teacher's Edition*, pp. 3A–3B.

STANDARDS FOR FOREIGN LANGUAGE LEARNING
Weiter geht's! *Pupil's Edition:* (2.2; 4.2) *Annotated Teacher's Edition:* (1.2; 3.2)

Teacher's Name _____ Class _____ Date _____

KAPITEL 1 · Das Land am Meer (Wiederholungskapitel)

Zweite Stufe (pp. 16–23)

Activities in the shaded boxes enhance the basic lesson and are ideal for **block scheduling**.

Lesson Plans

Objectives
Students will review asking and telling what they may or may not do, asking for information, inquiring about someone's health and responding, asking about and expressing pain, and expressing hope.

Motivate
See Teaching Suggestion, p. 30.

Teach
1. Have students read **Fit ohne Fleisch**, p. 16, and do Activity 20, p. 16.
2. Present **Wortschatz**, p. 17. See Presentation, p. 3P.
3. Play the audio recording for Activity 21, p. 17 *(Audio CD 1)*, and check for comprehension.
   Have students do Communicative Activity 1-3, *Activities for Communication*, pp. 3–4.
4. Present **So sagt man das!** *(Asking and telling what you may or may not do)*, p. 17.
5. Have students pair off to do Activity 22, p. 18.
6. Present **So sagt man das!** *(Asking for information)* and **Ein wenig Grammatik** *(The forms of dieser and welcher)*, p. 18. See Presentation, p. 3P.
   Have students do Activity 11, *Grammar and Vocabulary Worksheets*, p. 6.
7. Have students pair off to do Activity 23, p. 18.
8. Present **Wortschatz**, p. 18. See Presentation, p. 3P.
9. Play the audio recording for Activity 24, p. 19 *(Audio CD 1)*, and check for comprehension.
10. Present **Wortschatz** and **Und dann noch ...**, p. 19. See Presentation, p. 3Q.
11. Present **So sagt man das!** *(Inquiring about someone's health and responding; asking about and expressing pain)*, p. 20. See Presentation, p. 3Q. Present also **Ein wenig Grammatik** *(Reflexive pronouns)*, p. 20.
    Have students do Activity 7a, *Practice and Activity Book*, p. 10.
12. Play the audio recording for Activity 26, p. 20 *(Audio CD 1)*, and check for comprehension.
13. Present **So sagt man das!** *(Expressing hope)*, p. 20. See Presentation, p. 3Q.
14. Have students do Activities 27-29, pp. 20–21.
    Show the video clip **Junge Sportler**, *Video Program (Videocassette 1)*. See Activity Master 1, *Video Guide*, p. 5.
15. Present **Landeskunde**, pp. 22–23. Have students do Activities 1 and 2, p. 23.

Additional Practice Options for Zweite Stufe
- *Grammar and Vocabulary Worksheets*, pp. 5–9
- Situation 1-2 Interview and Role-playing, *Activities for Communication*, pp. 113–114
- Additional Listening Activities 1-4, 1-5, and 1-6, *Listening Activities*, pp. 9–10 *(Audio CD 1)*
- Realia 1-2, *Activities for Communication*, p. 52
- Teaching Transparency 1-2, *Teaching Transparencies*
- Additional Grammar Practice, *Pupil's Edition*, Activities 4-8, pp. R41–R42

Close
Close, p. 3Q

Assess
Quiz 1-2A or 1-2B, *Testing Program*, pp. 5–8, and/or Performance Assessment, p. 3R

Resources
For correlated print and audiovisual materials, see *Annotated Teacher's Edition*, pp. 3A–3B.

STANDARDS FOR FOREIGN LANGUAGE LEARNING

Zweite Stufe *Pupil's Edition:* (1.1; 1.3; 2.1; 4.1; 5.1) *Annotated Teacher's Edition:* (3.1; 5.1)

14 Lesson Planner Komm mit! Level 3

Copyright © by Holt, Rinehart and Winston. All rights reserved.

Teacher's Name _____ Class _____ Date _____

Das Land am Meer (Wiederholungskapitel)
Ending the chapter (pp. 24–27)

Activities in the shaded boxes enhance the basic lesson and are ideal for **block scheduling**.

Lesson Plans

Zum Lesen

Objectives
Students will learn to use time lines to aid comprehension.

Prereading
- Do Motivating Activity, p. 3R, and read and discuss **Lesetrick**, p. 24.
- Have students do Activity 1, p. 24.
- Play the audio recording of **Eine alltägliche Verwirrung** *(Audio CD 1)*.

Reading
- Have students do Activities 2-4, p. 24. See Teaching Suggestion, p. 3R.
- Have students pair off to do Activities 5-8, pp. 24–25. See Thinking Critically: Analyzing, p. 3S.

Postreading
- Replay the audio recording of **Eine alltägliche Verwirrung** *(Audio CD 1)*. Compare students' earlier impressions with their current understanding of the story.
- Have students do Activities 9 and 10, p. 25.
- See Closure, p. 3S.
- For additional reading practice, see *Practice and Activity Book*, pp. 12–13.

Zum Schreiben

Objectives
Students will learn to brainstorm and freewrite to develop ideas.

- Do Motivating Activity, p. 3N, and read and discuss **Schreibtip**, p. 13.
- Have students do Activities A-C, p. 13. See the related suggestions, pp. 3M–3N.

Ending the chapter

Objectives
Students will assess their achievement of the chapter objectives and review the vocabulary in preparation for the Chapter Test.

- Have students do **Kann ich's wirklich?**, p. 26, individually or with a partner.
- Have students review the vocabulary in **Wortschatz**, p. 27.
- Show **Videoclips: Werbung**, *Video Program (Videocassette 1)*. See Activity Master 2, *Video Guide*, p. 6.

Assessment
- Chapter Test, *Testing Program*, pp. 9–14
- *Test Generator*, Chapter 1
- Suggested Project, *Annotated Teacher's Edition*, p. 3H
- Speaking Test, *Testing Program*, p. 295
- *Alternative Assessment Guide*, pp. 16 and 30

Resources
For correlated print and audiovisual materials, see *Annotated Teacher's Edition*, pp. 3A–3B.

STANDARDS FOR FOREIGN LANGUAGE LEARNING
Zum Lesen *Pupil's Edition:* (3.2) *Annotated Teacher's Edition:* (1.1; 2.2; 3.2; 5.2)
Zum Schreiben *Pupil's Edition:* (3.1) *Annotated Teacher's Edition:* (1.3)
Ending the Chapter *Pupil's Edition:* (5.1; 5.2) *Annotated Teacher's Edition:* (1.3; 5.1; 5.2)

Komm mit! Level 3 Lesson Planner **15**

Copyright © by Holt, Rinehart and Winston. All rights reserved.

Teacher's Name _____   Class _____   Date _____

Auf in die Jugendherberge (Wiederholungskapitel)

KAPITEL 2

Beginning the chapter (pp. 27A–31)

Activities in the shaded boxes enhance the basic lesson and are ideal for **block scheduling**.

Lesson Plans

Chapter Opener

- Do Motivating Activity, p. 27I.
- Have students look at photo #1, p. 28. See Building on Previous Skills, Background Information, and Teaching Suggestion, p. 27I.
- To review previously learned vocabulary, ask students to replace the suggested activity in the caption of photo #1 with another one that they might suggest in the same situation.
- Have students look at photo #2, p. 29. See the related Thinking Critically: Drawing Inferences, p. 27I.
- Call students' attention to the verb form **wär** in the caption of photo #2. Ask them if they recognize it, and if so, how they think the umlaut changes the meaning of **war.**
- Have students look at photo #3, p. 29. See the related Thinking Critically: Drawing Inferences, p. 27I.
- See Focusing on Outcomes, p. 27I.

Los geht's!

Objectives
Students will listen to a group of friends plan a trip.

- Do Motivating Activity, p. 27J.
- Play the audio recording of **Auf nach Thüringen!**, *(Audio CD 2)*. See Background Information, p. 27J.
- Have students answer the questions in Activity 1, p. 31.
- As an alternative to Activity 1 or for a slower pace, have students make a chart in which they list in a column under the heading **Wer?** the names of the characters in **Auf nach Thüringen!** Next to the names they should make two more columns, one labeled **Was?** and the other headed **Warum?** Play the audio recording of **Auf nach Thüringen!** and have students fill in their chart, noting what each person wants to do and why.
- Have students do Activities 2 and 3, p. 31.
- You might have students pair off to do Activity 3, p. 31, as a contest. The partners who finish first raise their hands and the game stops. If the answers are incorrect, resume play until another pair raise their hands, and so on.
- Have students do Activity 4, p. 31.
- To help students decide on a destination, you might replay the video of the Location Opener **Die neuen Bundesländer**, pp. 1–3, *Video Program (Videocassette 1)*.
- See Closure, p. 27J.
- Have students do Activity 1, *Practice and Activity Book*, p. 14.

Resources
For correlated print and audiovisual materials, see *Annotated Teacher's Edition*, pp. 27A–27B.

STANDARDS FOR FOREIGN LANGUAGE LEARNING
Chapter Opener *Pupil's Edition:* (4.2) *Annotated Teacher's Edition:* (2.2; 4.2)
Los geht's! *Pupil's Edition:* (1.2) *Annotated Teacher's Edition:* (1.1)

16 Lesson Planner   Komm mit! Level 3

Teacher's Name _____ Class _____ Date _____

KAPITEL 2

Auf in die Jugendherberge (Wiederholungskapitel)

Erste Stufe (pp. 32–37)

Activities in the shaded boxes enhance the basic lesson and are ideal for **block scheduling**.

Lesson Plans

Objectives
Students will review asking for and making suggestions, expressing preference and giving a reason, expressing wishes, and expressing doubt, conviction, and resignation.

Motivate
See Game, p. 27K.

Teach
1. Have students read **Willkommen!**, p. 32, and do Activity 5, p. 32.
2. Present **Wortschatz,** p. 33. See Presentation. p. 27K.
   Have students do Activities 1 and 2, *Grammar and Vocabulary Worksheets*, p. 10.
3. Play the recording for Activity 6, p. 33 *(Audio CD 2)*, and check for comprehension.
4. Present **So sagt man das!** *(Asking for and making suggestions)*, p. 33. See Presentation, p. 27K.
   Have students do Activity 2, *Practice and Activity Book*, pp. 15–16.
5. Have students pair off to do Activities 7 and 8, p. 34.
6. Play the recording for Activity 9, p. 34 *(Audio CD 2)*, and check for comprehension.
   Have students do Communicative Activity 2-2, *Activities for Communication*, pp. 5–6.
7. Play the recording for Activity 13, p. 35 *(Audio CD 2)*, and check for comprehension.
8. Present **So sagt man das!** *(Expressing preference and giving a reason)*, p. 35.
   Have students do Activity 4, *Grammar and Vocabulary Worksheets*, p. 12.
9. Have students pair off to do Activity 14, p. 36.
10. Present **So sagt man das!** *(Expressing wishes)*, p. 36. See Presentation, p. 27L.
11. Have students pair off to do Activity 16, p. 36.
    Have students work in groups to do Activity 17, p. 36.
12. Present **So sagt man das!** *(Expressing doubt, conviction, and resignation)*, p. 36.
13. Play the recording for Activity 18, p. 37 *(Audio CD 2)*, and check for comprehension.
14. Have students pair off to do Activity 19, p. 37.
    Show the video clip **Freizeit**, *Video Program (Videocassette 1)*. See *Video Guide*, p. 9.

Additional Practice Options for Erste Stufe
- *Grammar and Vocabulary Worksheets*, pp. 10–13
- *Practice and Activity Book*, pp. 15–18
- Communicative Activities 2-1 and 2-2, *Activities for Communication*, pp. 5–6
- Situation 2-1 Interview and Role-playing, *Activities for Communication*, pp. 115–116
- Additional Listening Activities 2-1, 2-2, and 2-3, *Listening Activities*, pp. 15–16 *(Audio CD 2)*
- Realia 2-1, *Activities for Communication*, p. 56
- Teaching Transparencies 2-1 and 2-2, *Teaching Transparencies*
- Additional Grammar Practice, *Pupil's Edition*, Activities 1–5, pp. R43–R44

Close
Close, p. 27M.

Assess
Quiz 2-1A or 2-1B, *Testing Program*, pp. 23–26, and/or Performance Assessment, p. 27M.

Resources
For correlated print and audiovisual materials, see *Annotated Teacher's Edition*, pp. 27A–27B.

STANDARDS FOR FOREIGN LANGUAGE LEARNING
Erste Stufe *Pupil's Edition:* (1.1; 1.3; 5.1) *Annotated Teacher's Edition:* (1.2; 2.1; 5.1)

Komm mit! Level 3   Lesson Planner **17**

Copyright © by Holt, Rinehart and Winston. All rights reserved.

Teacher's Name _____ Class _____ Date _____

Auf in die Jugendherberge (Wiederholungskapitel)

Weiter geht's! (pp. 40–44)

Activities in the shaded boxes enhance the basic lesson and are ideal for **block scheduling**.

Lesson Plans

Weiter geht's!

Objectives
Students will listen as German students make detailed plans for their trip to Weimar.

- Do Motivating Activity, p. 27M.
- Create four groups. Assign each group one of the characters in **Auf nach Thüringen!**, pp. 30–31. Tell each group to listen carefully to the **Los geht's!** episode to determine the personality of their assigned character, how the person interacts with the others in the conversation, where the person wants to go, what the person wants to do, and so on. Play the audio recording of **Auf nach Thüringen!** (Audio CD 2) and have students listen with their books closed. Have each group prepare a description of their character and his or her wishes. Then have a spokesperson from each group present the character to the class. Encourage the other groups to disagree with or add to what one group reports.
- Play the audio recording of **Auf nach Thüringen!**, pp. 30–31 (Audio CD 2). Ask students what they think the results of Frank's phone call will be and what the group will eventually decide to do. Note the suggestions on the board or on a transparency to compare later with the **Weiter geht's!** episode. See Thinking Critically: Drawing Inferences, p. 27M.
- Have students read to themselves the questions in Activity 22, p. 39, before they listen to the audio recording or read **Auf nach Weimar!**
- Play the audio recording of **Auf nach Weimar!** (Audio CD 2) as students read along in their books. See Teaching Suggestions and Culture Note, p. 27M.
- Have students do Activities 22 and 23, p. 39.
- To extend Activity 23, p. 39, ask students to read aloud the lines of someone in **Auf nach Weimar!** who expresses impatience, of someone who is sarcastic, of someone who is playing the role of mediator, and of someone who is teasing.
- Have students match lines from the conversation with the photos.
- Have students do Activity 24, p. 39.
- Have students identify the objects in the picnic basket and name the fruit pictured on p. 39. Ask them what else they would add to the picnic basket.
- See Closure, p. 27N.
- Have students do Activities 1 and 2, *Practice and Activity Book*, p. 19.

Resources
For correlated print and audiovisual materials, see *Annotated Teacher's Edition*, pp. 27A–27B.

STANDARDS FOR FOREIGN LANGUAGE LEARNING
Weiter geht's! *Pupil's Edition:* (2.2; 4.2) *Annotated Teacher's Edition:* (5.1)

18 Lesson Planner

Komm mit! Level 3

Copyright © by Holt, Rinehart and Winston. All rights reserved.

Teacher's Name _____ Class _____ Date _____

Auf in die Jugendherberge (Wiederholungskapitel)

Zweite Stufe (pp. 40–45)
Activities in the shaded boxes enhance the basic lesson and are ideal for **block scheduling**.

 Lesson Plans

Objectives
Students will review asking for information and expressing an assumption, expressing hearsay, asking for, making, and responding to suggestions, and expressing wishes when shopping.

Motivate
See Thinking Critically: Drawing Inferences, p. 27N.

Teach
1. Have students read **Jugendgästehaus Weimar** and do Activity 25, p. 40.
2. Present **Wortschatz,** p. 41. See Presentation, p. 27O.
3. Play the recording for Activity 26, p. 41 *(Audio CD 2)*, and check for comprehension.
4. Present **So sagt man das!** *(Asking for information and expressing an assumption)*, p. 41.
5. Have students pair off to do Activity 27, p. 41. See Teaching Suggestion, p. 27O.
   Have students do Communicative Activity 2-3, *Activities for Communication,* pp. 7–8.
6. Present **So sagt man das!** *(Expressing hearsay)*, p. 42. See Presentation, p. 27O.
7. Have students write Activity 29, p. 42, in class or for homework.
8. Present **So sagt man das!** *(Asking for, making, and responding to suggestions)*, p. 42.
9. Play the recording for Activity 30, p. 42 *(Audio CD 2)*, and check for comprehension.
10. Have students work in groups to do Activity 32, p. 43.
11. Present **Wortschatz,** p. 43. See Presentation, p. 27P.
    Have students do Activities 6 and 7, *Practice and Activity Book,* pp. 22–23.
12. Play the recording for Activity 33, p. 43 *(Audio CD 2)*, and check for comprehension.
13. Present **Ein wenig Grammatik** *(Adjective endings)*, p. 44. See Presentation, p. 27P.
14. Have students pair off to do Activity 34, pp. 43–44.
15. Present **So sagt man das!** *(Expressing wishes when shopping)*, p. 44. See Presentation, p. 27P.
    Have students do Activities 15 and 16, *Grammar and Vocabulary Worksheets,* p. 18.
16. Have students pair off to do Activity 35, p. 44.
17. Present **Landeskunde** and have students do questions 1-4, p. 45.
18. Have students write Activity 37, p. 44, using information from **Landeskunde,** p. 45.

Additional Practice Options for Zweite Stufe
- *Grammar and Vocabulary Worksheets,* pp. 14–18
- *Practice and Activity Book,* pp. 20–24
- Communicative Activities 2-3 and 2-4, *Activities for Communication,* pp. 7–8
- Situation 2-2 Interview and Role-playing, *Activities for Communication,* pp. 115–116
- Additional Listening Activities 2-4, 2-5, and 2-6, *Listening Activities,* pp. 16–18 *(Audio CD 2)*
- Realia 2-2, *Activities for Communication,* p. 57
- Teaching Transparencies 2-1 and 2-2, *Teaching Transparencies*
- Additional Grammar Practice, *Pupil's Edition, Activities 6-8,* pp. R44–R45

Close
Close, p. 27Q

Assess
Quiz 2-3A or 2-3B, *Testing Program,* pp. 35–38, and/or Performance Assessment, p. 27T

Resources
For correlated print and audiovisual materials, see *Annotated Teacher's Edition,* pp. 27A–27B.

STANDARDS FOR FOREIGN LANGUAGE LEARNING
Zweite Stufe *Pupil's Edition:* (1.1; 1.3; 2.1; 4.1) *Annotated Teacher's Edition:* (1.1)

Komm mit! Level 3   Lesson Planner **19**

Teacher's Name _____ Class _____ Date _____

KAPITEL 2 — Auf in die Jugendherberge (Wiederholungskapitel)

Ending the chapter (pp. 46–51)

Activities in the shaded boxes enhance the basic lesson and are ideal for **block scheduling**.

Lesson Plans

Zum Lesen

Objectives
Students will learn to derive the main idea from supporting details.

Prereading
- Do Motivating Activity, p. 27R, and read and discuss **Lesetrick,** p. 46.
- Have students do Activity 1, p. 46.

Reading
- Play the audio recording of the poems and have students do Activity 2, p. 46.
- Have students work in pairs or groups to do Activities 3-12, pp. 46–48. See the related Background Information and Teaching Suggestions, p. 27R.

Postreading
- Have students do Activity 13, p. 48.
- See Closure, p. 27S.
- For additional reading practice, see *Practice and Activity Book,* p. 25.

Zum Schreiben

Objectives
Students will learn to select appropriate information in order to write effectively about an unfamiliar topic.

- Read and discuss **Schreibtip,** p. 49.
- Have students do Activities A-C, p. 49. See the related suggestions, p. 27T.

Ending the chapter

Objectives
Students will assess their achievement of the chapter objectives and review the vocabulary in preparation for the Chapter Test.

- Have students do **Kann ich's wirklich?**, p. 50, individually or with a partner.
- Have students review the vocabulary in **Wortschatz,** p. 51.
- Show **Videoclips: Werbung,** *Video Program (Videocassette 1)*. See Activity Master 2, *Video Guide,* p. 10.

Assessment
- Chapter Test, *Testing Program,* pp. 31–36
- *Test Generator,* Chapter 2
- Speaking Test, *Testing Program,* p. 295
- *Alternative Assessment Guide,* pp. 17 and 31
- Suggested Project, *Annotated Teacher's Edition,* p. 27H

Resources
For correlated print and audiovisual materials, see *Annotated Teacher's Edition,* pp. 27A–27B.

STANDARDS FOR FOREIGN LANGUAGE LEARNING

Zum Lesen *Pupil's Edition:* (3.2) *Annotated Teacher's Edition:* (2.2; 3.2; 4.1; 4.2; 5.2)
Zum Schreiben *Pupil's Edition:* (3.1) *Annotated Teacher's Edition:* (5.1)
Ending the Chapter *Pupil's Edition:* (3.1; 5.1; 5.2) *Annotated Teacher's Edition:* (1.3; 5.1; 5.2)

Lesson Planner — Komm mit! Level 3

Copyright © by Holt, Rinehart and Winston. All rights reserved.

Teacher's Name _____ Class _____ Date _____

Aussehen: wichtig oder nicht?

Beginning the chapter (pp. 51A–55)

Activities in the shaded boxes enhance the basic lesson and are ideal for **block scheduling**.

Lesson Plans

Chapter Opener

- Do Motivating Activity, p. 51I.
- Have students read the introduction on p. 53 and answer briefly the questions it contains.
- Have students look at photo #1, p. 52. See For Individual Needs: Visual Learners, p. 51I.
- As students look at photo #1, p. 52, ask them who they think the people are, where they might be, and how they look.
- Have students look at photo #2, p. 53. See the related Teaching Suggestion, p. 51I.
- Have students look at photo #3, p. 53. See Building on Previous Skills, p. 51I.
- Ask students what type of store is pictured in photo #3, p. 53, and what they see in the photo that supports their response.
- See Focusing on Outcomes, p. 51I.

Los geht's!

Objectives
Students will listen to four German students talk about appearance.

- Do Motivating Activity, p. 51J.
- Draw on the board the chart shown in Activity 1a, p. 55. Play the audio recording of **Gut aussehen** *(Audio CD 3)*. When the recording ends, ask students what they can remember about the four German students in each of the four categories. Write their suggestions in the chart on the board.
- Replay the audio recording of **Gut aussehen**. Have students make additions or corrections to the chart on the board.
- Have students do Activity 1b, p. 55.
- Extend Activity 1b, p. 55, by asking students to note three things that Tanja says she does to lift her spirits.
- Have students pair off to do Activity 3, p. 55.
- Have students write Activity 2, p. 55. See the related Teaching Suggestion, p. 51J.
- For a slower pace with Activity 2, p. 55, tell students to copy any sentences from **Gut aussehen** that apply to their own feelings and actions. Tell them to adapt the sentences if necessary and arrange them in a paragraph about themselves.
- See Closure, p. 51J.
- Show the video clip **Gesund essen**, *Video Program (Videocassette 1)*. See Activity Master 1, *Video Guide*, p. 13.

Resources
For correlated print and audiovisual materials, see *Annotated Teacher's Edition*, pp. 51A–51B.

STANDARDS FOR FOREIGN LANGUAGE LEARNING

Chapter Opener *Pupil's Edition:* (4.1; 4.2) *Annotated Teacher's Edition:* (4.1; 4.2)
Los geht's! *Pupil's Edition:* (1.2) *Annotated Teacher's Edition:* (5.1)

Teacher's Name _____ Class _____ Date _____

KAPITEL 3 — Aussehen: wichtig oder nicht?

Erste Stufe (pp. 56–61)

Activities in the shaded boxes enhance the basic lesson and are ideal for **block scheduling.**

Lesson Plans

Objectives
Students will learn to ask for and express opinions.

Motivate
See Teaching Suggestion, p. 51K.

Teach
1. Have students read and take **Ein Fitnesstest,** p. 56.
2. Present **Wortschatz,** p. 56. See Presentation, p. 51K.
   Have students do Activity 1, *Practice and Activity Book,* p. 28.
3. Play the recording for Activity 4, p. 57 *(Audio CD 3)* and check for comprehension.
4. Have students pair off to do Activity 5, p. 57.
   Have students do Communicative Activity 3-2, *Activities for Communication,* pp. 9–10.
5. Have students do Activity 6, p. 57. See the related Teaching Suggestion, p. 51L.
   Show Teaching Transparency 3-2, *Teaching Transparencies,* and have students tell what actions the girl is considering to lift her spirits.
6. Present **So sagt man das!** *(Asking for and expressing opinions),* p. 57.
7. Play the audio recording for Activity 7, p. 57 *(Audio CD 3),* and check for comprehension.
   Have students do Activity 3, *Grammar and Vocabulary Worksheets,* p. 20.
8. Have students pair off to do Activity 8, p.58.
9. Present **Grammatik** *(Da- and wo-compounds),* p. 58. See Presentation, p. 51L.
   Have students do Activities 6-8, *Practice and Activity Book,* pp. 30–31.
10. Have students do Activities 9 and 10, pp. 58–59.
11. Have students write Activity 13, p. 59, and then work in groups to do Activity 12, p. 59.
12. Do Motivating Activity for **Landeskunde,** p. 51M. Present **Landeskunde,** p. 61.
13. Have students do Activities A and B, p. 61.
    Have students do Activities 1-3, *Practice and Activity Book,* p. 32.

Additional Practice Options for Erste Stufe
- *Grammar and Vocabulary Worksheets,* pp. 19–22
- *Practice and Activity Book,* pp. 28–32
- Communicative Activities 3-1 and 3-2, *Activities for Communication,* pp. 9–10
- Situation 3-1 Interview and Role-playing, *Activities for Communication,* pp. 117–118
- Additional Listening Activities 3-1, 3-2, and 3-3, *Listening Activities,* pp. 23–24 *(Audio CD 3)*
- Realia 3-1 and 3-2, *Activities for Communication,* pp. 61–62
- Teaching Transparencies 3-1 and 3-2, *Teaching Transparencies*
- Additional Grammar Practice, *Pupil's Edition,* Activities 1-5, pp. R46–R47

Close
Close, p. 51M

Assess
Quiz 3-1A or 3-1B, *Testing Program,* pp. 45–48, and/or Performance Assessment, p. 51N

Resources
For correlated print and audiovisual materials, see *Annotated Teacher's Edition,* pp. 51A–51B.

STANDARDS FOR FOREIGN LANGUAGE LEARNING

Erste Stufe *Pupil's Edition:* (1.1; 1.3; 2.1; 4.1) *Annotated Teacher's Edition:* (1.1; 1.2)

Teacher's Name _____ Class _____ Date _____

KAPITEL 3

Aussehen: wichtig oder nicht?

Weiter geht's! (pp. 62–63)

Activities in the shaded boxes enhance the basic lesson and are ideal for **block scheduling**.

Lesson Plans

Weiter geht's!

Objectives
Students will listen as four German students discuss fashion.

- Do Motivating Activity, p. 51 N.
- Replay the audio recording of **Gut aussehen,** pp. 54–55 *(Audio CD 3)*, and have students listen with their books closed. As they listen to Philipp, Sonja, Tanja, and Michael talk, have them note only the comments the speakers make about clothing and fashion. Discuss their findings.
- Play the audio recording of **Immer mit der Mode. Oder?** *(Audio CD 3)* as students listen with their books closed. Tell them to listen for the gist of each speaker's remarks. Then check for comprehension.
- Have students listen again to the audio recording as they read along in their books. See the related Teaching Suggestion, p. 51 N.
- Have students do Activity 16, p. 63. See Group Work, p. 51 N.
- Have students do Activity 17, p. 63. See the related Teaching Suggestion, p. 51 N.
- For listening practice before students write Activity 17, p. 63, read aloud the fifteen descriptive sentences and have students try to identify the person each sentence describes.
- For further practice, once students have identified which speaker fits each sentence in Activity 17, p. 63, have them restate or rewrite each sentence, changing the subject to **ich** and making any necessary changes.
- Have students do Activity 18, p. 63. See For Individual Needs: Auditory Learners, p. 51 O.
- As an extension of Activity 18, p. 63, ask students to put together an outfit they think one of the friends would wear by cutting pictures of clothing from magazines. Ask them to write on a separate piece of paper a description of the outfit to accompany their collage. Display the pictures, read aloud at random the written descriptions, and have students try to guess which outfits you are describing.
- Have students pair off to do Activity 19, p. 63.
- For further challenge with **Immer mit der Mode. Oder?**, compose two incoherent paragraphs, each one consisting of quotations from the four friends that represent conflicting points of view. Distribute copies to students and ask them to rewrite the two paragraphs so that each one is coherent and states only one point of view.
- See Closure, p. 51 O.
- Have students do Activities 1 and 2, *Practice and Activity Book*, p. 33.

Resources
For correlated print and audiovisual materials, see *Annotated Teacher's Edition*, pp. 51A–51B.

STANDARDS FOR FOREIGN LANGUAGE LEARNING
Weiter geht's! *Pupil's Edition:* (2.2; 4.2) *Annotated Teacher's Edition:* (5.1)

Komm mit! Level 3   Lesson Planner

Teacher's Name _____ Class _____ Date _____

KAPITEL 3 Aussehen: wichtig oder nicht?

Zweite Stufe (pp. 64–68)

Activities in the shaded boxes enhance the basic lesson and are ideal for **block scheduling**.

Lesson Plans

Objectives
Students will learn to express sympathy and resignation, give advice, give a reason, admit something, and express regret.

Motivate
See Teaching Suggestion, p. 51O.

Teach
1. Present **Wortschatz**, p. 65. See Presentation, p. 51O.
   Have students do Activities 8 and 9, *Grammar and Vocabulary Worksheets*, p. 23.
2. Present **So sagt man das!** *(Expressing sympathy and resignation)*, p. 65. See Presentation, p. 51P.
3. Have students read **Eine Freundin gibt Rat**, p. 64, and do Activity 20, p. 65.
4. Have students pair off to do Activity 21, p. 65.
5. Present **So sagt man das!** *(Giving advice)*, p. 66. See Presentation, p. 51P.
   Have students do Activity 11, *Grammar and Vocabulary Worksheets*, p. 24.
6. Play the recording for Activity 22, p. 66 *(Audio CD 3)*, and check for comprehension.
7. Have students pair off to do Activity 23, p. 66.
   Have students do Communicative Activity 3-3, *Activities for Communication*, pp. 11–12.
8. Present **Grammatik** *(Infinitive clauses)*, p. 67. See Presentation, p. 51P.
9. Have students work in groups to do Activity 25, p. 67.
10. Present **So sagt man das!** *(Giving a reason)*, p. 67. See Presentation, p. 51P.
    Have students do Activity 4, *Practice and Activity Book*, p. 35.
11. Have students pair off to do Activity 26, p. 68.
12. Present **So sagt man das!** *(Admitting something and expressing regret)*, p. 68.
    Have students do Activity 7, *Practice and Activity Book*, pp. 36–37.
13. Have students pair off to do Activity 27, p. 68. See Teacher Note, p. 51Q.
14. Have students write Activity 28, p. 68, in class or for homework.

Additional Practice Options for Zweite Stufe
- *Grammar and Vocabulary Worksheets*, pp. 23–27
- *Practice and Activity Book*, pp. 34–37
- Communicative Activities 3-3 and 3-4, *Activities for Communication*, pp. 11–12
- Situation 3-2 Interview and Role-playing, *Activities for Communication*, pp. 117–118
- Additional Listening Activities 3-4, 3-5, and 3-6, *Listening Activities*, pp. 24–26 *(Audio CD 3)*
- Realia 3-3, *Activities for Communication*, p. 63
- Teaching Transparencies 3-1 and 3-2, *Teaching Transparencies*
- Additional Grammar Practice, *Pupil's Edition*, Activities 6-8, pp. R47–R48

Close
Close, p. 51Q

Assess
Quiz 3-2A or 3-2B, *Testing Program*, pp. 49–52, and/or Performance Assessment, p. 51Q

Resources
For correlated print and audiovisual materials, see *Annotated Teacher's Edition*, pp. 51A–51B.

STANDARDS FOR FOREIGN LANGUAGE LEARNING
Zweite Stufe *Pupil's Edition:* (1.1; 4.1) *Annotated Teacher's Edition:* (1.2; 1.3; 4.1)

24 Lesson Planner   Komm mit! Level 3

Copyright © by Holt, Rinehart and Winston. All rights reserved.

Teacher's Name _____ Class _____ Date _____

KAPITEL 3 — Aussehen: wichtig oder nicht?

Ending the chapter (pp. 69–75)

Activities in the shaded boxes enhance the basic lesson and are ideal for **block scheduling**.

Lesson Plans

Zum Schreiben

Objectives
Students will learn to organize their ideas.

- Do Motivating Activity, p. 51Q, and read and discuss **Schreibtip**, p. 69.
- Have students do Activities A-C, p. 69. See the related suggestions, pp. 51Q–51R.

Zum Lesen

Prereading
- Do Motivating Activity, p. 51R, and read and discuss **Lesetrick**, p. 70.
- Have students do Activities 1-3, p. 70.

Reading
- Have students do Activities 4-9, pp. 70–71. See Teacher Notes and Teaching Suggestions, pp. 51R–51S.
- Have students do Activities 10 and 11, p. 71. See Thinking Critically: Analyzing, p. 51R.

Postreading
- Have students do Activity 12, p. 71.
- For additional reading practice, see *Practice and Activity Book,* pp. 38–39.

Anwendung

Objectives
Students will review and integrate all four skills and culture in preparation for the Chapter Test.

- Have students respond to the survey in Activity 1a, p. 72.
- Play the recording for Activity 1b, p. 73 *(Audio CD 3),* and have students check their answers.
- Have students write Activity 1c, p. 73.
- **Have groups write additional true/false statements concerning nutrition and exchange their surveys with other groups.**
- Have students do Activities 2 and 3, p. 73.
- Have students do **Kann ich's wirklich?**, p. 74, individually or with a partner.
- Have students review **Wortschatz,** p. 75. See Games, p. 51T.
- Show **Videoclips: Werbung,** *Video Program (Videocassette 1).* See Activity Master 2, *Video Guide,* p. 14.

Assessment
- Chapter Test, *Testing Program,* pp. 53–58
- *Test Generator,* Chapter 3
- Speaking Test, *Testing Program,* p. 296
- *Alternative Assessment Guide,* pp. 18 and 32
- Suggested Project, *Annotated Teacher's Edition,* p. 51H

Resources
For correlated print and audiovisual materials, see *Annotated Teacher's Edition,* pp. 51A–51B.

STANDARDS FOR FOREIGN LANGUAGE LEARNING
Zum Schreiben Pupil's Edition: (3.1) Annotated Teacher's Edition: (3.1)
Zum Lesen Pupil's Edition: (3.2) Annotated Teacher's Edition: (3.2; 4.2; 5.2)
Anwendung Pupil's Edition: (1.3; 5.1; 5.2) Annotated Teacher's Edition: (1.2; 1.3; 5.2)

Komm mit! Level 3 — Lesson Planner 25

Teacher's Name _____ Class _____ Date _____

KAPITEL 4
Verhältnis zu anderen

Beginning the chapter (pp. 75A–83)

Activities in the shaded boxes enhance the basic lesson and are ideal for **block scheduling**.

Lesson Plans

Location Opener

Objectives
Students will learn about famous people, historical events, and places in Würzburg.

- Have students read the Location Opener, pp. 76–79.
- Have students do the Pre-viewing Activity, *Video Guide*, p. 16.
- Show **Komm mit nach Würzburg!**, *Video Program (Videocassette 1)*.
- Have students do the Viewing Activity, *Video Guide*, p. 16. See Background Information, p. 75A.
- See the Post-viewing Suggestions, *Video Guide*, p. 15.

Chapter Opener

- Do Motivating Activity, p. 79I.
- Have students look at photo #1, p. 80. See For Individual Needs: Visual Learners, p. 79I.
- Have students look at photo #2, p. 81. See the related Teaching Suggestion, p. 79I.
- Have students try to guess the meaning of the caption.
- Have students look at photo #3, p. 81. See the related Teaching Suggestion, p. 79I.
- Referring to the caption of photo #3, p. 81, ask students what the purpose or function of the father's remark is. Have them complete his statement with different advice.
- See Focusing on Outcomes, p. 79I.

Los geht's!

Objectives
Students will listen to German students talk about their relationships with friends and family.

- Do Motivating Activity, p. 79J.
- Have students copy the chart in Activity 1, p. 83.
- Play the audio recording of the first part of **Verhältnis zu Eltern und Freunden** *(Audio CD 4)*. Have students fill in the column labeled **Eltern** in their charts.
- Play the audio recording of the second part of **Verhältnis zu Eltern und Freunden** *(Audio CD 4)*. Have students fill in the column labeled **Freunden**.
- Play the audio recording of the rest of **Verhältnis zu Eltern und Freunden** *(Audio CD 4)*. Ask students what contact Michael and Tanja have had with former schoolmates and apprentices and how Sonja explains this lack of contact.
- Have students read **Verhältnis zu Eltern und Freunden**, pp. 82–83.
- Have students answer the questions in Activity 1, p. 83.
- Have students do Activities 2 and 3, p. 83.
- See Closure, p. 79J.
- Have students do Activities 1 and 2, *Practice and Activity Book*, p. 40.

Resources
For correlated print and audiovisual materials, see *Annotated Teacher's Edition*, pp. 79A–79B.

STANDARDS FOR FOREIGN LANGUAGE LEARNING

Location Opener   *Pupil's Edition:* (3.1; 4.2) *Annotated Teacher's Edition:* (3.1; 5.1)
Chapter Opener   *Pupil's Edition:* (4.2) *Annotated Teacher's Edition:* (1.2; 3.2; 4.2)
Los geht's!   *Pupil's Edition:* (1.2) *Annotated Teacher's Edition:* (1.1; 5.1)

Teacher's Name _____ Class _____ Date _____

Verhältnis zu anderen

Erste Stufe (pp. 84–87)

Activities in the shaded boxes enhance the basic lesson and are ideal for **block scheduling**.

Lesson Plans

Objectives
Students will learn to agree.

Motivate
See Teaching Suggestion, p. 79K.

Teach
1. Present **Wortschatz**, p. 84. See Presentation, p. 79K.
   Have students do Activity 1, *Grammar and Vocabulary Worksheets*, p. 28.
2. Have students write Activity 4, p. 84.
3. Play the audio recording for Activity 5, p. 85 *(Audio CD 4)*, and check for comprehension.
4. Have students pair off to do Activity 6, p. 85.
   For further practice talking or writing about relationships with parents, show Teaching Transparency 4-1, *Teaching Transparencies*.
5. Present **So sagt man das!** *(Agreeing)*, p. 85. See Presentation, p. 79K.
6. Play the audio recording for Activity 7, p. 85 *(Audio CD 4)*, and check for comprehension.
7. Have students pair off to do Activity 8, p. 85.
   Have students do Communicative Activity 4-2, *Activities for Communication*, pp. 15–16.
8. Present **Ein wenig Landeskunde**, p. 86. See Presentation, p. 79L.
9. Have student read the chart entitled **Mit wem verbringen Jugendliche ihre Freizeit?** See Teacher Note, p. 79L.
10. Present **Ein wenig Grammatik** *(Ordinal numbers)*, p. 86. See Presentation, p. 79K.
11. Have students do Activity 9, p. 86.
    Have students do Activity 4, *Practice and Activity Book*, p. 42.
12. Have students write Activity 10, p. 86, in class or for homework.
13. Present **Grammatik** *(Relative clauses)*, p. 87. See Presentation, p. 79L.
14. Have students write Activity 11, p. 87.
    Show the video clip **Im Freizeitzentrum,** *Video Program (Videocassette 1)*. See Activity Master 1, *Video Guide*, p. 19.

Additional Practice Options for Erste Stufe
- *Grammar and Vocabulary Worksheets*, pp. 28–31
- *Practice and Activity Book*, pp. 41–44
- Communicative Activities 4-1 and 4-2, *Activities for Communication*, pp. 13–16
- Situation 4-1 Interview and Role-playing, *Activities for Communication*, pp. 119–120
- Additional Listening Activities 4-1, 4-2, and 4-3, *Listening Activities*, pp. 31–32 *(Audio CD 4)*
- Teaching Transparency 4-1, *Teaching Transparencies*
- Additional Grammar Practice, *Pupil's Edition, Activities* 1-3, pp. R48–R49

Close
Close, p. 79M

Assess
Quiz 4-1A or 4-1B, *Testing Program*, pp. 67–70, and/or Performance Assessment, p. 79M

Resources
For correlated print and audiovisual materials, see *Annotated Teacher's Edition*, pp. 79A–79B.

STANDARDS FOR FOREIGN LANGUAGE LEARNING

Erste Stufe *Pupil's Edition:* (1.1; 2.2; 4.1) *Annotated Teacher's Edition:* (1.2; 4.2)

Komm mit! Level 3   Lesson Planner **27**

Copyright © by Holt, Rinehart and Winston. All rights reserved.

Teacher's Name _____ Class _____ Date _____

KAPITEL 4

Verhältnis zu anderen

Weiter geht's! (pp. 88–89)

Activities in the shaded boxes enhance the basic lesson and are ideal for **block scheduling**.

Lesson Plans

Weiter geht's!

Objectives
Students will listen as four German students talk about their relationships with different types of people.

- Do Motivating Activity, p. 79M, in which students talk about the diversity of their classmates.
- Replay the audio recording of **Verhältnis zu Eltern und Freunden,** pp. 82–83 *(Audio CD 4)*, and have students listen with their books closed. As they listen, have them try to discern how well Philipp, Sonja, Tanja, and Michael get along with parents and friends. Then, on that basis, have them predict what the attitude of the four would be toward fringe groups and foreigners. Note their predictions, which may be confirmed or disproved later after they hear **Verhältnis zu anderen Leuten.**
- Have students listen with their books closed as you play the first half of the audio recording of **Verhältnis zu anderen Leuten** *(Audio CD 4),* including the interviewer's first question and the responses regarding fringe groups at school. Tell them to listen for the gist of each speaker's remarks. Discuss their findings.
- Have students listen as you play the second half of the audio recording of **Verhältnis zu anderen Leuten** *(Audio CD 4),* including the interviewer's question and the responses regarding foreign students at school. Tell them to listen carefully to determine the attitude of each speaker toward these students. Discuss their findings.
- Have students listen again to the audio recording of **Verhältnis zu anderen Leuten** *(Audio CD 4)* as they read along in their books. See the related Teaching Suggestions and Language Note, p. 79M.
- Have students do Activity 12, p. 89.
- Have students add to the chart they made for Activity 1 of **Los geht's!,** p. 83. They should make two additional columns, labeled **Randgruppen** and **Ausländer,** and fill in the attitudes of Michael, Tanja, Philipp, and Sonja toward these groups.
- Have students do Activity 13, p. 69.
- Have students describe the photos on pp. 88 and 89.
- For further practice, replay the audio recording of **Verhältnis zu anderen Leuten.** Pause the recording just before the last clause or phrase of each person's remark and have students try to finish it.
- For further challenge with **Verhältnis zu anderen Leuten,** have the entire class or small groups reread the conversation, changing it as they read to refer to their own school population.
- See Closure, p. 79M.
- Have students do Activity 1, *Practice and Activity Book,* p. 45.

Resources
For correlated print and audiovisual materials, see *Annotated Teacher's Edition,* pp. 79A–79B.

STANDARDS FOR FOREIGN LANGUAGE LEARNING
Weiter geht's! *Pupil's Edition:* (2.2; 4.2) *Annotated Teacher's Edition:* (2.1; 5.1)

28 Lesson Planner

Komm mit! Level 3

Copyright © by Holt, Rinehart and Winston. All rights reserved.

Teacher's Name _____ Class _____ Date _____

Verhältnis zu anderen

Zweite Stufe (pp. 90–94)

Activities in the shaded boxes enhance the basic lesson and are ideal for **block scheduling**.

Lesson Plans

Objectives
Students will learn to give advice, introduce another point of view, and hypothesize.

Motivate
See the related Teaching Suggestion, p. 79N.

Teach
1. Present **Wortschatz,** p. 90. See Presentation, p. 79N.
2. Play the audio recording for Activity 14, p. 90 *(Audio CD 4)*, and check for comprehension.
   Have students read the letters in Realia 4-1, *Activities for Communication*, p. 66.
3. Have students work in groups to do Activity 15, p. 90.
4. Present **So sagt man das!** *(Giving advice; introducing another point of view)*, p. 91.
5. Play the audio recording for Activity 16, p. 91 *(Audio CD 4)*, and check for comprehension.
6. Have students pair off to do Activities 17 and 18, p. 91.
7. Present **So sagt man das!** *(Hypothesizing)*, p. 92. See Presentation, p. 79O.
8. Present **Ein wenig Grammatik** *(Using hätte and wäre in place of würde haben and würde sein)*, p. 92.
   See Presentation and Music Connection, p. 79O.
   Have students do Activity 8, *Grammar and Vocabulary Worksheets*, p. 34.
9. Play the audio recording for Activity 19, p. 92 *(Audio CD 4)*, and check for comprehension.
10. Have students do Activity 20, p. 92.
    Show Teaching Transparency 4-2, *Teaching Transparencies*. Ask students to assume the role of a person in one of the scenes and say what they would do if they were that person.
11. Present **Grammatik,** *(The genitive case)*, p. 93. See Presentation, p. 79O.
12. Have students write Activity 22, p. 93. See Teacher Note, p. 79O.
    Have students do Activities 3 and 5, *Practice and Activity Book*, pp. 47, 48.
13. Have students write Activity 23, p. 93, in class or for homework.
14. Have students read **Landeskunde** and do Activities A and B, p. 94.
    Have students do Activities 1-3, *Practice and Activity Book*, p. 50.

Additional Practice Options for Zweite Stufe
- *Grammar and Vocabulary Worksheets*, pp. 32–36
- *Practice and Activity Book*, pp. 46–50
- Situation 4-2 Interview and Role-playing, *Activities for Communication*, pp. 119–120
- Additional Listening Activities 4-4, 4-5, and 4-6, *Listening Activities*, pp. 32–34 *(Audio CD 4)*
- Realia 4-1, 4-2, and 4-3, *Activities for Communication*, pp. 66–68
- Teaching Transparency 4-2, *Teaching Transparencies*
- Additional Grammar Practice, *Pupil's Edition*, Activities 4-5, pp. R49–R50

Close
Close, p. 79P

Assess
Quiz 4-2A or 4-2B, *Testing Program*, pp. 71–74, and/or Performance Assessment, p. 79Q

Resources
For correlated print and audiovisual materials, see *Annotated Teacher's Edition*, pp. 79A–79B.

STANDARDS FOR FOREIGN LANGUAGE LEARNING
Zweite Stufe *Pupil's Edition:* (1.1; 1.3; 2.1; 4.1) *Annotated Teacher's Edition:* (2.2; 3.1; 4.1; 4.2; 5.1)

Komm mit! Level 3   Lesson Planner
Copyright © by Holt, Rinehart and Winston. All rights reserved.

Teacher's Name _____ Class _____ Date _____

KAPITEL 4 — Verhältnis zu anderen

Ending the chapter (pp. 95–103)

Activities in the shaded boxes enhance the basic lesson and are ideal for **block scheduling**.

Lesson Plans

Zum Schreiben

Objectives
Students will learn to determine the purpose of their writing.

- Do Motivating Activity, p. 79Q, and read and discuss **Schreibtip**, p. 95.
- Have students do Activities A-C, p. 95. See the related suggestions, pp. 79Q–79R.

Zum Lesen

Objectives
Students will learn to determine the main idea of a story.

Prereading
- Do Motivating Activity, p. 79R.
- Read and discuss **Lesetrick**, p. 96.

Reading
- Have students do Activities 1-5, pp. 96–97. See Teacher Notes, p. 79R.
- Have students do Activities 6-10, pp. 98–99. See the related Teaching Suggestion, p. 79R.

Postreading
- Have students do Activities 11 and 12, p. 99.
- See Closure, p. 79S.
- For additional reading practice, see *Practice and Activity Book*, pp. 51–52.

Anwendung

Objectives
Students will review and integrate all four skills and culture in preparation for the Chapter Test.

- Play the audio recording for Activity 1, p. 100 *(Audio CD 4)*, and check for comprehension.
- Have students do Activities 2-4, pp. 100–101.
- Have students work in groups to do Activity 5, p. 101. See Teaching Suggestion, p. 79T.
- Have students do **Kann ich's wirklich?**, p. 102, individually or with a partner.
- Have students review the vocabulary in **Wortschatz**, p. 103.
- Show **Videoclips: Werbung**, *Video Program (Videocassette 1)*. See Teaching Suggestions, *Video Guide*, p. 18, and Activity Master 2, *Video Guide*, p. 20.

Assessment
- Chapter Test, *Testing Program*, pp. 75–80
- Test Generator, Chapter 4
- Suggested Project, *Annotated Teacher's Edition*, p. 79H
- Speaking Test, *Testing Program*, p. 296
- Alternative Assessment Guide, pp. 19 and 33

Resources
For correlated print and audiovisual materials, see *Annotated Teacher's Edition*, pp. 79A–79B.

STANDARDS FOR FOREIGN LANGUAGE LEARNING
Zum Schreiben Pupil's Edition: (3.1) Annotated Teacher's Edition: (1.3)
Zum Lesen Pupil's Edition: (3.2) Annotated Teacher's Edition: (3.2; 4.2; 5.2)
Anwendung Pupil's Edition: (5.1; 5.2) Annotated Teacher's Edition: (1.1; 1.3; 2.2; 3.1)

Teacher's Name _____ Class _____ Date _____

KAPITEL 5 — Rechte und Pflichten

Beginning the chapter (pp. 103A–107)

Activities in the shaded boxes enhance the basic lesson and are ideal for **block scheduling**.

Lesson Plans

Chapter Opener

- Do Motivating Activity, p. 103I.
- Have students read the introductory paragraph at the top of p. 105. See the first Teaching Suggestion, p. 103I.
- Have students look at photo #1, p. 104. See the related Thinking Critically: Drawing Inferences, p. 103I.
- Have students identify the documents on p. 104 and relate them to the theme of the chapter as expressed in the title. Also, ask them if they can name the countries whose flags are shown on p. 104.
- Have students look at photo #2, p. 105. See the related Teaching Suggestion, p. 103I.
- As students look at photo #2, p. 105, ask them how old they think the students are, where they are, what they are doing, and what time of year it is.
- Have students look at photo #3, p. 105. See Background Information, For Individual Needs: Visual Learners, and Community Link, p. 103I.
- As students look at photo #3, p. 105, ask them what opportunities for service are available to young people in the United States.
- See Focusing on Outcomes, p. 103I.

Los geht's!

Objectives

Students will listen to German teenagers as they talk about the rights and responsibilities that come with adulthood.

- Do Motivating Activity, p. 103J.
- Have students read **Mit achtzehn darf man alles. Oder?** See Teaching Suggestion, p. 103J.
- Ask students if Martin's friends' description of the American requirements for a driver's license is true or not and to modify it if necessary.
- Have students do Activities 1 and 2, p. 107.
- Before students answer question #3 in Activity 2, p. 107, show the video clip **In einer Fahrschule,** *Video Program (Videocassette 1),* in which a driving instructor and some students talk about the cost of getting a driver's license and the differences between getting a license in Germany and getting one in the United States. See Teaching Suggestions, *Video Guide, p. 22,* and Activity Master 1, *Video Guide, p. 23.*
- See Closure, p. 103J.
- Have students do Activities 1 and 2, *Practice and Activity Book,* p. 53.

Resources

For correlated print and audiovisual materials, see *Annotated Teacher's Edition,* pp. 103A–103B.

STANDARDS FOR FOREIGN LANGUAGE LEARNING

Chapter Opener *Pupil's Edition:* (3.2; 4.2) *Annotated Teacher's Edition:* (2.1)
Los geht's! *Pupil's Edition:* (1.2) *Annotated Teacher's Edition:* (1.2; 4.2)

Komm mit! Level 3 — Lesson Planner **31**

Copyright © by Holt, Rinehart and Winston. All rights reserved.

Teacher's Name _____ Class _____ Date _____

KAPITEL 5: Rechte und Pflichten

Erste Stufe (pp. 108–111)

Activities in the shaded boxes enhance the basic lesson and are ideal for **block scheduling**.

Lesson Plans

Objectives
Students will learn to talk about what is possible and to say what they would have liked to do.

Motivate
See Teaching Suggestion, p. 103K.

Teach
1. Have students read the article from the constitution and **Was bedeutet das?**, p. 108.
   Show Teaching Transparency 5-1, *Teaching Transparencies*. Have students select a statement from **Was bedeutet das?** that each teen might say.
2. Present **Wortschatz**, p. 108. See Presentation, p. 103K.
3. Play the audio recording for Activity 3, p. 109 *(Audio CD 5)*, and check for comprehension.
4. Present **So sagt man das!** *(Talking about what is possible)* and **Ein wenig Grammatik** *(The könnte forms)*, p. 109. See Presentations, p. 103L.
   Have students do Activities 1, 5, and 6, *Practice and Activity Book*, pp. 54, 56.
5. Play the audio recording for Activity 4, p. 109 *(Audio CD 5)*, and check for comprehension.
6. Have students do Activities 5 and 6, pp. 109–110.
   Have students do Communicative Activity 5-2, *Activities for Communication*, pp. 17–18.
7. Present **So sagt man das!** *(Saying what you would have liked to do)*, p. 110.
8. Present **Grammatik** *(Further uses of wäre and hätte)*, p. 110.
   Have students do Activities 7 and 8, *Grammar and Vocabulary Worksheets*, p. 40.
9. Have students pair off to do Activity 7, p. 110.
10. Have students do Activities 9 and 10, p. 111.
    An alternative procedure for Activity 10, p. 111, would be to assign each group one of the topics to discuss and then have reporters summarize their group's discussion for the class.
11. Have students write Activity 11, p. 111, in class or for homework.

Additional Practice Options for Erste Stufe
- *Grammar and Vocabulary Worksheets*, pp. 37–40
- *Practice and Activity Book*, pp. 54–57
- Communicative Activities 5-1 and 5-2, *Activities for Communication*, pp. 17–18
- Situation 5-1 Interview and Role-playing, *Activities for Communication*, pp. 121–122
- Additional Listening Activities 5-1, 5-2, and 5-3, *Listening Activities*, pp. 39–40 *(Audio CD 5)*
- Realia 5-1 and 5-2, *Activities for Communication*, pp. 71–72
- Teaching Transparency 5-1, *Teaching Transparencies*
- Additional Grammar Practice, *Pupil's Edition*, Activities 1-3, pp. R50–R51

Close
Close, p. 103L

Assess
Quiz 5-1A or 5-1B, *Testing Program*, pp. 89–92, and/or Performance Assessment, p. 103M

Resources
For correlated print and audiovisual materials, see *Annotated Teacher's Edition*, pp. 103A–103B.

STANDARDS FOR FOREIGN LANGUAGE LEARNING

Erste Stufe *Pupil's Edition:* (1.1; 1.2; 1.3; 4.1) *Annotated Teacher's Edition* (1.1)

Teacher's Name _____ Class _____ Date _____

Rechte und Pflichten

KAPITEL 5

Weiter geht's! (pp. 112–114)

Activities in the shaded boxes enhance the basic lesson and are ideal for **block scheduling**.

Lesson Plans

Weiter geht's!

Objectives
Students will listen as four young people give their opinions of military and civil service.

- Do Motivating Activity, p. 103M.
- Have students listen with their books closed as you play the audio recording of **Die Wehrpflicht: dafür oder dagegen?** *(Audio CD 5)*. Write key words on the board as suggested in Teaching Suggestion, p. 103M. Tell students to listen for the opinions of the four young people regarding 1) compulsory military service for men, 2) military service for women, and 3) optional civil service. Discuss their findings.
- Have students listen again to the audio recording of **Die Wehrpflicht: dafür oder dagegen?** as they read along in their book. Have them add to or correct their initial findings.
- As an alternative procedure, form four groups. One group is responsible for understanding and relating the opinions of Martin, another group focuses on the views of Stefan, and a third group listens for the opinions of Julia and Angie. The fourth group will act as judge. Play the audio recording of **Die Wehrpflicht: dafür oder dagegen?** As the first three groups present the views of their assigned character(s), the fourth group adds to or corrects what the other groups relate.
- Have students reread **Die Wehrpflicht: dafür oder dagegen?**, pp. 112–113. Tell them to find and note statements in the conversation wherein the speakers interrupt, express surprise, speculate or wonder, express doubt, express resignation, give an opinion, make certain of what they heard someone say, concede a point to someone, agree, relate hearsay, express indignation, and express relief. Check their results.
- Have students do Activity 12, p. 113.
- For further challenge, have students make a list of transitional words they find in **Die Wehrpflicht: dafür oder dagegen?** that they can use in later discussions involving the exchange of differing points of view.
- Have students describe the photos on pp. 112 and 113.
- See Closure, p. 103M.
- Introduce some vocabulary for **Landeskunde**, p. 114. See the related Teaching Suggestion, p. 103N.
- Have students read **Gleichberechtigung** in **Landeskunde**, p. 114, and answer the questions.
- Have students do Activities 1-4, *Practice and Activity Book*, p. 59.
- Show the video clip **Der Zivildienst**, *Video Program (Videocassette 1)*. See Activity Master 2, *Video Guide*, p. 24.
- Have students discuss the feasibility of national **Zivildienst** in the United States. Ask them what young people might do if **Zivildienst** were instituted here.
- Have students do Activities 1 and 2, *Practice and Activity Book*, p. 58.

Resources
For correlated print and audiovisual materials, see *Annotated Teacher's Edition*, pp. 103A–103B.

STANDARDS FOR FOREIGN LANGUAGE LEARNING
Weiter geht's! *Pupil's Edition:* (2.1; 2.2; 4.2) *Annotated Teacher's Edition:* (4.2)

Komm mit! Level 3 — Lesson Planner

Teacher's Name _____ Class _____ Date _____

KAPITEL 5

Rechte und Pflichten

Zweite Stufe (pp. 115–119)

Activities in the shaded boxes enhance the basic lesson and are ideal for **block scheduling**.

Lesson Plans

Objectives
Students will learn to say that something is going on right now, report past events, and express surprise, relief, and resignation.

Motivate
See the related Teaching Suggestion, p. 103N.

Teach
1. Present **Wortschatz**, p. 115. See Presentation, p. 103O.
   Have students do Activity 3, *Practice and Activity Book*, p. 61.
2. Present **So sagt man das!** *(Saying that something is going on right now)*, p. 115. See Presentation, p. 103O. Present also **Ein wenig Grammatik** *(Verbs used as neuter nouns)*, p. 116.
   Have students do Communicative Activity 5-3, *Activities for Communication*, pp. 19–20.
3. Have students pair off to do Activity 13, p. 116.
4. Present **Ein wenig Landeskunde,** p. 116. See Presentation, p. 103O.
5. Present **So sagt man das!** *(Reporting past events)*, p. 116. See Presentation, p. 103O.
6. Play the audio recording for Activity 14, p. 117 *(Audio CD 5)*, and check for comprehension.
7. Present **Grammatik** *(The past tense - imperfect of modals)*, p. 117.
   Have students do Activities 13 and 14, *Grammar and Vocabulary Worksheets*, pp. 43–44.
8. Have students pair off to do Activity 15, p. 117.
9. Present **Wortschatz**, p. 118. See Presentation, p. 103P.
10. Have students pair off to do Activity 16, p. 118.
11. Present **So sagt man das!** *(Expressing surprise, relief, and resignation)*, p. 118.
12. Play the recording for Activity 17, p. 118 *(Audio CD 5)*, and check for comprehension.
13. Have students pair off to do Activity 18, p. 118.
    Have students do Activities 4 and 7, *Practice and Activity Book*, pp. 61, 62.
14. Have students pair off to do Activity 20, p. 118.
15. Have students write Activity 22, p. 119, in class or for homework.

Additional Practice Options for Zweite Stufe
- *Grammar and Vocabulary Worksheets*, pp. 41–45
- *Practice and Activity Book*, pp. 60–63
- Communicative Activities 5-3 and 5-4, *Activities for Communication*, pp. 19–20
- Situation 5-2 Interview and Role-playing, *Activities for Communication*, pp. 121–122
- Additional Listening Activities 5-4, 5-5, and 5-6, *Listening Activities*, pp. 40–42 *(Audio CD 5)*
- Realia 5-3, *Activities for Communication*, p. 73
- Teaching Transparency 5-2, *Teaching Transparencies*
- Additional Grammar Practice, *Pupil's Edition*, Activities 4-6, pp. R51–R52

Close
Close, p. 103P

Assess
Quiz 5-2A or 5-2B, *Testing Program*, pp. 93–96, and/or Performance Assessment, p. 103P

Resources
For correlated print and audiovisual materials, see *Annotated Teacher's Edition*, pp. 103A–103B.

STANDARDS FOR FOREIGN LANGUAGE LEARNING
Zweite Stufe *Pupil's Edition:* (1.1; 1.3; 2.2; 4.1) *Annotated Teacher's Edition:* (1.3; 5.1)

Teacher's Name _____ Class _____ Date _____

KAPITEL 5 — Rechte und Pflichten

Ending the chapter (pp. 120–127)

Activities in the shaded boxes enhance the basic lesson and are ideal for **block scheduling**.

Lesson Plans

Zum Lesen

Objectives
Students will learn to determine the purpose of a reading selection before they read.

Prereading
- Do Motivating Activity, p. 103Q.
- Read and discuss **Lesetrick**, p. 120, and have students do Activities 1-3, pp. 120–121.

Reading
- Have students read the excerpts from Hitler's speeches, p. 120, and do Activities 5-7, pp. 121–122.
- Have students read **Das letzte Flugblatt**, p. 121, and do Activities 8-10, p. 122.
- Have students read **Verführt von dummen, mörderischen Sprüchen**, p. 122, and do Activity 11, p. 122.

Postreading
- Have students do Activity 12, p. 122.
- See Closure, p. 103R.

Zum Schreiben

Objectives
Students will learn to ask questions in order to gather ideas.

- Do Motivating Activity, p. 103S, and read and discuss **Schreibtip**, p. 123.
- Have students do Activities A-C, p. 123. See the related suggestions, pp. 103S–103T.

Anwendung

Objectives
Students will review and integrate all four skills and culture in preparation for the Chapter Test.

- Play the audio recording for Activity 1, p. 124 *(Audio CD 5)*, and check for comprehension.
- Have students draw the chart shown in Activity 3, p. 124, read Activity 2, p. 124, and fill in the chart.
- Have students do Activities 4 and 5, p. 125; have students write Activity 7, p. 125.
- Have students do **Kann ich's wirklich?**, p. 126, individually or with a partner.
- Have students review the vocabulary in the **Wortschatz**, p. 127. See Game, p. 103T.
- Show **Videoclips: Werbung**, *Video Program (Videocassette 1)*. See Activity Master 2, *Video Guide*, p. 24.

Assessment
- Chapter Test, *Testing Program*, pp. 97–102
- *Test Generator*, Chapter 5
- Suggested Project, *Annotated Teacher's Edition*, p. 103H
- Speaking Test, *Testing Program*, p. 297
- *Alternative Assessment Guide*, pp. 20 and 34

Resources
For correlated print and audiovisual materials, see *Annotated Teacher's Edition*, pp. 103A–103B.

STANDARDS FOR FOREIGN LANGUAGE LEARNING
Zum Lesen *Pupil's Edition:* (3.2) *Annotated Teacher's Edition:* (2.2; 3.2)
Zum Schreiben *Pupil's Edition:* (3.1) *Annotated Teacher's Edition:* (1.1; 1.3)
Anwendung *Pupil's Edition:* (5.1; 5.2) *Annotated Teacher's Edition:* (3.1)

Teacher's Name _____ Class _____ Date _____

KAPITEL 6
Medien: stets gut informiert?

Beginning the chapter (pp. 127A–131)

Activities in the shaded boxes enhance the basic lesson and are ideal for **block scheduling**.

Lesson Plans

Chapter Opener

- Do Motivating Activity, p. 127I.
- Have students look at photo #1, p. 128. See the related Teaching Suggestions, p. 127I.
- Have students look at photo #2, p. 129. See the related Teaching Suggestion, p. 127I.
- Review types of TV programs by having students repeat the caption of photo #2, p. 129, substituting other programs in the sentence. See Level 2 *Pupil's Edition*, p. 240.
- Call students' attention to photo #3, p. 129. See Thinking Critically: Drawing Inferences, p. 127I.
- See Focusing on Outcomes, p. 127I.
- See Thinking Critically: Comparing and Contrasting, p. 127I.

Los geht's!

Objectives
Students will listen to young people talk about the German media.

- Do Motivating Activity, p. 127J.
- Before presenting **Die Macht der Medien**, pp. 130–131, you might choose to present **Wortschatz**, p. 132, which introduces new vocabulary that students will encounter in **Los geht's!**
- Play the audio recording of **Die Macht der Medien** *(Audio CD 6)* and have students read along in their books on pp. 130–131.
- Assign each character in **Die Macht der Medien** to a group. Replay the audio recording of **Die Macht der Medien** and have each group listen carefully to their assigned character's remarks to determine the person's point of view and reasons for it. Then have the groups summarize their character's position(s).
- For additional listening practice, quote at random the advantages of the different media stated in **Die Macht der Medien** and ask students to identify the media the remarks support.
- Have students do Activities 1 and 2, p. 131. See Cooperative Learning, p. 127J.
- Ask students if they read only the **Sensationspresse** and only the headlines as Frank believes. Ask them what they think of the tabloids.
- See Closure, p. 127J.
- Have students do Activities 1 and 2, *Practice and Activity Book*, p. 66.

Resources
For correlated print and audiovisual materials, see *Annotated Teacher's Edition*, pp. 127A–127B.

STANDARDS FOR FOREIGN LANGUAGE LEARNING

Chapter Opener *Pupil's Edition:* (4.1; 4.2) *Annotated Teacher's Edition:* (3.1)
Los geht's! *Pupil's Edition:* (1.2) *Annotated Teacher's Edition:* (1.2; 3.2; 5.2)

Teacher's Name _____ Class _____ Date _____

KAPITEL 6: Medien: stets gut informiert?

Erste Stufe (pp. 132–137)

Activities in the shaded boxes enhance the basic lesson and are ideal for **block scheduling**.

Lesson Plans

Objectives
Students will learn to ask someone to take a position, ask for reasons, express opinions, report past events, agree or disagree, change the subject, and interrupt.

Motivate
See Teaching Suggestion, p. 127K.

Teach
1. Have students read **Zahl des Tages** and **Die TV-Kids,** p. 132, and do Activity 3, p. 133.
2. Present **Wortschatz,** p. 132. See Presentation, p. 127K.
   Have students do Activities 1 and 2, *Grammar and Vocabulary Worksheets,* p. 46.
3. Play the audio recording for Activity 4, p. 133 *(Audio CD 6),* and check for comprehension.
4. Present **So sagt man das!** *(Asking someone to take a position; asking for reasons; expressing opinions),* p. 133. See Presentation, p. 127L.
   Have students do Communicative Activity 6-1, *Activities for Communication,* pp. 21–22.
5. Play the audio recording for Activity 5, p. 133 *(Audio CD 6),* and check for comprehension.
6. Have students work in groups to do Activity 7, p. 134.
7. Present **So sagt man das!** *(Reporting past events),* p. 134, and **Grammatik** *(Narrative past, imperfect),* pp. 134–135. See Presentations, p. 127L.
8. Have students do Activity 9, p. 135.
9. Have students work in groups to do Activity 10, p. 136.
10. Present **So sagt man das!** *(Agreeing and disagreeing; changing the subject; interrupting),* p. 136.
    Have students do Activity 6, *Grammar and Vocabulary Worksheets,* p. 50.
11. Play the audio recording for Activity 11, p. 136 *(Audio CD 6),* and check for comprehension.
12. Have students work in groups to do Activity 12, p. 136.
    Show the video clip **Über Kinos und Videos,** *Video Program (Videocassette 1).*
13. Present **Landeskunde,** p. 137. See the related Teaching Suggestions, p. 127M.
14. Have students do Activities 1-4, p. 137.

Additional Practice Options for Erste Stufe
- *Grammar and Vocabulary Worksheets,* pp. 46–50
- *Practice and Activity Book,* pp. 67–71
- Communicative Activities 6-1 and 6-2, *Activities for Communication,* pp. 21–22
- Situation 6-1 Interview and Role-playing, *Activities for Communication,* pp. 123–124
- Additional Listening Activities 6-1, 6-2, and 6-3, *Listening Activities,* pp. 47–48 *(Audio CD 6)*
- Realia 6-1, *Activities for Communication,* p. 76
- Teaching Transparency 6-1, *Teaching Transparencies*
- Additional Grammar Practice, *Pupil's Edition,* Activity 1, pp. R52–R53

Close
Close, p. 127M

Assess
Quiz 6-1A or 6-1B, *Testing Program,* pp. 111–114, and/or Performance Assessment, p. 127M

Resources
For correlated print and audiovisual materials, see *Annotated Teacher's Edition,* pp. 127A–127B.

STANDARDS FOR FOREIGN LANGUAGE LEARNING
Erste Stufe *Pupil's Edition:* (1.1; 1.3; 2.1; 4.1) *Annotated Teacher's Edition:* (1.1; 2.1; 4.1; 4.2)

Komm mit! Level 3

Teacher's Name _____ Class _____ Date _____

KAPITEL 6
Medien: stets gut informiert?

Weiter geht's! (pp. 138–139)

Activities in the shaded boxes enhance the basic lesson and are ideal for **block scheduling**.

Lesson Plans

Weiter geht's!

Objectives
Students will listen to German students talk about their work on the school newspaper.

- Do Motivating Activity, p. 127M.
- Have students listen with their books closed as you play the audio recording of the first half of **Unsere eigene Zeitung!** *(Audio CD 6)*, in which the editors of the school newspaper discuss their work. Have students listen carefully and note the pleasures and the frustrations of working on the newspaper that are mentioned by the speakers.
- Have students listen to the audio recording of the second half of **Unsere eigene Zeitung!**, in which a reporter for the school newspaper interviews two members of the student government. Tell students to listen carefully to learn the functions of the student government and one of its accomplishments.
- Have students listen to the audio recording of **Unsere eigene Zeitung!** in its entirety as they read along in their books. Have them make any additions or corrections to their initial findings.
- Have students pair off to do Activity 13, p. 139.
- To expand their answer to question #2 of Activity 13, p. 139, tell students to reread the **Landeskunde**, p. 137, to find additional functions of the student government.
- Have students do Activity 14, p. 139.
- For a slower pace with Activity 14, p. 139, replay the audio recording of **Unsere eigene Zeitung!** as students read along in their books. Pause the recording after each speaker's remarks. Ask students to identify the speaker's purpose(s), such as expressing surprise, interrupting, and so on. Have them repeat the phrase or sentence that reflects the function they identify.
- For further challenge, replay the audio recording of the second half of **Unsere eigene Zeitung!** Pause the recording after the interviewer's questions and have students answer them.
- Have students identify the people in the photos on pp. 138–139 and tell what they think they are doing and saying.
- For further challenge, form small groups and ask each group to adapt the interviews in **Unsere eigene Zeitung!** to reflect comparable situations in their own school or in an average American school.
- See Closure, p. 127N.
- Have students do Activities 1-3, *Practice and Activity Book*, p. 72.

Resources
For correlated print and audiovisual materials, see *Annotated Teacher's Edition*, pp. 127A–127B.

STANDARDS FOR FOREIGN LANGUAGE LEARNING
Weiter geht's! *Pupil's Edition:* (2.2; 4.2) *Annotated Teacher's Edition:* (4.2)

Teacher's Name _____ Class _____ Date _____

KAPITEL 6 — Medien: stets gut informiert?

Zweite Stufe (pp. 140–143)

Activities in the shaded boxes enhance the basic lesson and are ideal for **block scheduling**.

Lesson Plans

Objectives
Students will learn to express surprise or annoyance.

Motivate
See the related Teaching Suggestion, p. 127N.

Teach
1. Present **Wortschatz**, p. 140. See Presentation, p.127O.
2. Have students read **Leserbriefe an die Redaktion der Pepo** and do Activity 15, p. 140.
   Have students do Activities 7-9, *Grammar and Vocabulary Worksheets*, p. 51.
3. Play the audio recording for Activity 16, p. 141 *(Audio CD 6)*, and check for comprehension.
4. Present **So sagt man das!** *(Expressing surprise or annoyance)*, p. 141. See Presentation, p. 127O.
   Have students do Activities 4 and 7, *Practice and Activity Book*, pp. 74, 76.
5. Play the audio recording for Activity 17, p. 141 *(Audio CD 6)*, and check for comprehension.
6. Have students pair off to do Activity 18, p. 141.
7. Present **Grammatik** *(Superlative forms of adjectives)*, p. 142. See Presentation, p. 127O.
8. Have students do Activity 21, p. 143.
   Have students do Communicative Activity 6-3, *Activities for Communication*, pp. 23–24.
9. Have students pair off to do Activity 19, p. 142.
   Have students do Activity 9, *Practice and Activity Book*, p. 76.
10. Have students pair off to do Activity 20, p. 143.
11. Have students pair off to do Activity 22, p. 143. See the related Teaching Suggestion, p. 127O.
12. Present **Wortschatz**, p. 143. See Presentation, p.127O.
    Have students do Activities 3 and 6, *Practice and Activity Book*, pp. 74, 75.
13. Have students work in groups to do Activity 23, p. 143.

Additional Practice Options for Zweite Stufe
- *Grammar and Vocabulary Worksheets*, pp. 51–54
- *Practice and Activity Book*, pp. 73–76
- Communicative Activities 6-3 and 6-4, *Activities for Communication*, pp. 23–24
- Additional Listening Activities 6-4, 6-5, and 6-6, *Listening Activities*, pp. 49–50 *(Audio CD 6)*
- Realia 6-2 and 6-3, *Activities for Communication*, pp. 77–78
- Teaching Transparency 6-2, *Teaching Transparencies*
- Additional Grammar Practice, *Pupil's Edition*, Activities 2–4, p. R53

Close
Close, p. 127P

Assess
Quiz 6-2A or 6-2B, *Testing Program*, pp. 115–118, and/or Performance Assessment, p. 127P

Resources
For correlated print and audiovisual materials, see *Annotated Teacher's Edition*, pp. 127A–127B.

STANDARDS FOR FOREIGN LANGUAGE LEARNING
Zweite Stufe Pupil's Edition: (1.1; 1.3; 4.1) *Annotated Teacher's Edition:* (1.2)

Komm mit! Level 3

Teacher's Name _____ Class _____ Date _____

KAPITEL 6

Medien: stets gut informiert?

Ending the chapter (pp. 144–151)

Activities in the shaded boxes enhance the basic lesson and are ideal for **block scheduling**.

Lesson Plans

Zum Lesen
Objectives Students will learn to predict the outcome of a story.
Prereading • Do Motivating Activity, p. 127P. • Read and discuss **Lesetrick,** p. 144. **Reading** • Have students do Activities 1-8, pp. 144–146. **Postreading** • Have students do Activities 9 and 10, p. 146. • See Closure, p. 127Q. • For additional reading practice, see *Practice and Activity Book,* pp. 77–78.
Zum Schreiben
Objectives Students will learn to use an outline.
• Do Motivating Activity, p. 127R, and read and discuss **Schreibtip,** p. 147. • Have students do Activity A-C, p. 147. See the related suggestions, p. 127R.
Anwendung
Objectives Students will review and integrate all four skills and culture in preparation for the Chapter Test.
• Have students do Activity 1, p.148. • Play the audio recording for Activity 2, p. 148 *(Audio CD 6),* and check for comprehension. • Have students work in groups to do Activities 5 and 6, p. 149. See Group Work, p. 127S. • Have students write Activity 7, p. 149, in class or for homework. • Have students do **Kann ich's wirklich?,** p. 150, individually or with a partner. • Have students review the vocabulary in **Wortschatz,** p. 151. See Game, p. 127T. • Show **Videoclips: Werbung,** *Video Program (Videocassette 1).* See Activity Master 2, *Video Guide,* p. 28. **Assessment** • Chapter Test, *Testing Program,* pp. 119–124 • *Test Generator,* Chapter 6 • Speaking Test, *Testing Program,* p. 297 • *Alternative Assessment Guide,* pp. 21 and 35 • Suggested Project, *Annotated Teacher's Edition,* p. 127H
Resources For correlated print and audiovisual materials, see *Annotated Teacher's Edition,* pp. 127A–127B.
STANDARDS FOR FOREIGN LANGUAGE LEARNING **Zum Lesen** *Pupil's Edition:* (3.2) *Annotated Teacher's Edition:* (2.2; 3.2) **Zum Schreiben** *Pupil's Edition:* (3.1) *Annotated Teacher's Edition:* (5.1) **Anwendung** *Pupil's Edition:* (5.1; 5.2) *Annotated Teacher's Edition:* (4.2; 5.2)

Teacher's Name _____ Class _____ Date _____

KAPITEL 7
Ohne Reklame geht es nicht!

Beginning the chapter (pp. 151A–159)

Activities in the shaded boxes enhance the basic lesson and are ideal for **block scheduling**.

Lesson Plans

Location Opener

Objectives
Students will learn about famous people, historical events, and places in Frankfurt.

- Have students read **Komm mit nach Frankfurt!**, pp. 152–155. See Background Information, p. 151A.
- Have students do the Pre-viewing Activity, *Video Guide,* p. 30.
- Show **Komm mit nach Frankfurt!**, *Video Program (Videocassette 2).*
- Have students do the Viewing Activity, *Video Guide,* p. 30.
- See the Post-viewing Suggestions, *Video Guide,* p. 29.

Chapter Opener

- Do Motivating Activity, p. 155I.
- Have students look at photo #1, p. 156. See Thinking Critically: Analyzing/Drawing Inferences and Teacher Note, p. 155I.
- Have students look at photo #2, p. 157. See Language Note and Teaching Suggestion, p. 155I.
- Ask students what they think **Leerdammer** is. Have them answer the question posed by the caption.
- Have students look at photo #3, p. 157. See Thinking Critically: Drawing Inferences, p. 155I.
- Have students look at the products on pp. 156–157 and try to determine what they are.
- See Focusing on Outcomes, p. 155I.

Los geht's!

Objectives
Students will listen to German teenagers talk about advertising.

- Do Motivating Activity, p. 155J.
- Play the audio recording of **Werbung—ja oder nein?** *(Audio CD 7).* Have students listen with their books closed and then ask them to tell you what they understood of the interview.
- Replay the audio recording of **Werbung—ja oder nein?** and have students read along in their books as they listen. They should correct any initial misunderstandings.
- Have students do Activities 1 and 2, p. 159.
- See Closure, p. 155J.
- Have students do Activities 1 and 2, *Practice and Activity Book,* p. 79.

Resources
For correlated print and audiovisual materials, see *Annotated Teacher's Edition,* pp. 155A–155B.

STANDARDS FOR FOREIGN LANGUAGE LEARNING
Location Opener *Pupil's Edition:* (3.1; 4.2) *Annotated Teacher's Edition:* (3.1; 4.2; 5.2)
Chapter Opener *Pupil's Edition:* (3.2; 4.2) *Annotated Teacher's Edition:* (2.1; 3.2)
Los geht's! *Pupil's Edition:* (1.2) *Annotated Teacher's Edition:* (1.1; 1.2; 4.2; 5.1)

Teacher's Name _____ Class _____ Date _____

KAPITEL 7: Ohne Reklame geht es nicht!

Erste Stufe (pp. 160–165)

Activities in the shaded boxes enhance the basic lesson and are ideal for **block scheduling**.

Lesson Plans

Objectives
Students will learn to express annoyance and compare.

Motivate
See For Individual Needs: Visual Learners, p. 155K.

Teach
1. Have students read **Werbung—pro und contra,** p. 160. Discuss as a class the questions in the box.
2. Present **Wortschatz,** p. 160. See Presentation, p. 155K.
   Have students do Activities 1-3, *Grammar and Vocabulary Worksheets,* pp. 55–56.
3. Present **So sagt man das!** *(Expressing annoyance),* p. 161. See Presentation, p. 155L.
4. Play the audio recording for Activity 3, p. 161 *(Audio CD 7),* and check for comprehension.
5. Have students work in groups to do Activities 4 and 5, p. 161.
6. Present **So sagt man das!** *(Comparing),* p. 161. See Presentation, p. 155L.
7. Play the audio recording for Activity 6, p. 161 *(Audio CD 7),* and check for comprehension.
   Show the video clip **Ein großes Angebot,** *Video Program (Videocassette 2).* See Teaching Suggestions, *Video Guide,* p. 32, and Activity Master 1, *Video Guide,* p. 33.
8. Present **Grammatik** *(derselbe, der gleiche),* p. 162. See Presentation, p. 155L.
9. Have students work in groups to do Activity 8, p. 162.
10. Present **Grammatik** *(Adjective endings following determiners of quantity),* p. 163.
    Have students do Activity 4, *Practice and Activity Worksheets,* p. 81.
11. Have students pair off to do Activity 9, p. 163.
12. Play the audio recording for Activity 10, p. 163 *(Audio CD 7),* and check for comprehension.
13. Have students pair off to do Activities 12 and 13, p. 164.
    For further practice with slogans and ads, see Teaching Transparency 7-1, *Teaching Transparencies.*
14. Have students work as a class to do Activity 14, p. 164.
15. Have students write Activity 15, p. 164, in class or for homework.
16. Present **Landeskunde,** p. 165. See Teaching Suggestions, pp. 155M–155N.

Additional Practice Options for Erste Stufe
- *Grammar and Vocabulary Worksheets,* pp. 55–59
- *Practice and Activity Book,* pp. 80–84
- Communicative Activities 7-1 and 7-2, *Activities for Communication,* pp. 25–26
- Situation 7-1 Interview and Role-playing, *Activities for Communication,* pp. 125–126
- Additional Listening Activities 7-1, 7-2, and 7-3, *Listening Activities,* pp. 55–56 *(Audio CD 7)*
- Realia 7-2 and 7-3, *Activities for Communication,* pp. 82–83
- Teaching Transparency 7-1, *Teaching Transparencies*
- Additional Grammar Practice, *Pupil's Edition,* Activities 1-3, p. R54

Close
Close, p. 155N

Assess
Quiz 7-1A or 7-1B, *Testing Program,* pp. 147–150, and/or Performance Assessment, p. 155N

Resources
For correlated print and audiovisual materials, see *Annotated Teacher's Edition,* pp. 155A–155B.

STANDARDS FOR FOREIGN LANGUAGE LEARNING
Erste Stufe *Pupil's Edition:* (1.1; 1.3; 2.1; 4.1) *Annotated Teacher's Edition:* (2.1; 4.2; 5.2)

Teacher's Name _____ Class _____ Date _____

KAPITEL 7

Ohne Reklame geht es nicht!

Weiter geht's! (pp. 166–167)

Activities in the shaded boxes enhance the basic lesson and are ideal for **block scheduling**.

Lesson Plans

Weiter geht's!
Objectives Students will listen to German students discuss a particular TV advertisement.
• Do Motivating Activity, p. 155O. • Before presenting **Image-Werbung**, pp. 166–167, you might choose to present **Wortschatz**, p. 168, which includes new vocabulary that students will encounter in **Weiter geht's!** See Presentation, p. 155P. • Have students listen with their books closed as you read aloud or play the audio recording of the description of the commercial for the chocolate drink on p. 166. • Have students open their books and read the description of the commercial for the chocolate drink on p. 166. See Thinking Critically: Drawing Inferences, p. 155O. • Have students do #1 and #2 of Activity 16, p. 167. • Continue playing the audio recording of **Image-Werbung** *(Audio CD 7)*, in which the German class discusses commercials with the teacher. Pause after the teacher's first remark at the top of p. 167. Ask students if they agree with the German students about the role of children in commercials. • Have students listen to the remainder of the audio recording of **Image-Werbung**. Tell them to listen carefully for the German students' criticisms of commercials. • Have students do #4 of Activity 16, p. 167. • For a slower pace with #4 of Activity 16, p. 167, quote briefly the major points raised by the German class and have students express their agreement or disagreement. • Have students do #3 of Activity 16, p. 167. • Have students read the ad on p. 167 and identify the sponsor and the product(s) that are advertised. • Call students' attention to the column pictured on p. 167. Ask them what columns such as this are called **(Litfaßsäulen)** and what their purpose is. See Culture Notes, p. 155I. • For further challenge, have students write a description of their favorite commercial, patterned after the one on p. 166. • For further practice describing an ad, have students do Activity 5, *Practice and Activity Book*, p. 88. • See Closure, p. 155O. • Have students do Activity 1, *Practice and Activity Book*, p.85.
Resources For correlated print and audiovisual materials, see *Annotated Teacher's Edition*, pp. 155A–155B.

STANDARDS FOR FOREIGN LANGUAGE LEARNING
Weiter geht's! *Pupil's Edition:* (2.2; 4.2) *Annotated Teacher's Edition:* (4.2)

Komm mit! Level 3

Copyright © by Holt, Rinehart and Winston. All rights reserved.

Teacher's Name _____ Class _____ Date _____

KAPITEL 7: Ohne Reklame geht es nicht!

Zweite Stufe (pp. 168–171)

Activities in the shaded boxes enhance the basic lesson and are ideal for **block scheduling**.

Lesson Plans

Objectives
Students will learn to elicit agreement and agree and to express conviction, uncertainty, and what seems to be true.

Motivate
See the related Teaching Suggestion, p. 155P.

Teach
1. Present **Wortschatz,** p. 168. See Presentation, p. 155P.
   Have students do Communicative Activity 7-3, *Activities for Communication,* pp. 27–28.
2. Present **So sagt man das!** *(Eliciting agreement and agreeing),* p. 168. See Presentation, p. 155P.
3. Play the audio recording for Activity 17, p. 168 *(Audio CD 7),* and check for comprehension.
4. Have students pair off to do Activity 18, p. 169.
5. Present **Ein wenig Grammatik** *(Review of relative clauses with forms of der, die, das)* and **Grammatik** *(Introducing relative clauses with was and wo),* p. 169. See Presentation, p. 155P.
   Have students do Activities 12 and 13, *Grammar and Vocabulary Worksheets,* p. 62.
6. Have students pair off to do Activity 20, p. 170.
7. Have students do Activity 21, p. 170. See the related Teaching Suggestion, p. 155P.
8. Present **So sagt man das!** *(Expressing conviction, uncertainty, and what seems to be true),* p. 170.
   Have students do Activity 6, *Practice and Activity Book,* p. 88.
9. Play the audio recording for Activity 22, p. 170 *(Audio CD 7),* and check for comprehension.
10. Present **Grammatik** *(irgendein and irgendwelche),* p. 171. See Presentation, p. 155P.
11. Have students do Activity 23, p. 171.
12. Present **Wortschatz,** p. 171. See Presentation, p. 155Q.
    Have students do Activity 1, *Practice and Activity Book,* p. 86.
13. Have students pair off to do Activity 24, p. 171.
14. Have students work in groups to do Activity 25, p. 171.

Additional Practice Options for Zweite Stufe
- *Grammar and Vocabulary Worksheets,* pp. 60–63
- *Practice and Activity Book,* pp. 86–89
- Communicative Activities 7-3 and 7-4, *Activities for Communication,* pp. 27–28
- Situation 7-2 Interview and Role-playing, *Activities for Communication,* pp. 125–126
- Additional Listening Activities 7-4, 7-5, and 7-6, *Listening Activities,* pp. 56–58 *(Audio CD 7)*
- Realia 7-2 and 7-3, *Activities for Communication,* pp. 82–83
- Teaching Transparency 7-2, *Teaching Transparencies*
- Additional Grammar Practice, *Pupil's Edition,* Activities 4-7, p. R 55

Close
Close, p. 155Q

Assess
Quiz 7-2A or 7-2B, *Testing Program,* pp. 151–154, and/or Performance Assessment, p. 155Q

Resources
For correlated print and audiovisual materials, see *Annotated Teacher's Edition,* pp. 155A–155B.

STANDARDS FOR FOREIGN LANGUAGE LEARNING
Zweite Stufe *Pupil's Edition:* (1.1; 4.1) *Annotated Teacher's Edition:* (1.1; 4.1)

Teacher's Name _____ Class _____ Date _____

KAPITEL 7
Ohne Reklame geht es nicht!

Ending the chapter (pp. 172–179)

Activities in the shaded boxes enhance the basic lesson and are ideal for **block scheduling**.

Lesson Plans

Zum Lesen

Objectives
Students will learn to use pictures and print type as clues to meaning.

Prereading
- Do Motivating Activity, p. 155R, and read and discuss **Lesetrick,** p. 172.
- Have students do Activities 1 and 2, pp. 172–173. See Teaching Suggestions, p. 155R.

Reading
- Have students do Activities 3-9, pp. 173–174.

Postreading
- Have students do Activity 10, p. 174. See the related Teacher Note, p. 155R.
- See Closure, p. 155R.
- For additional reading practice, see *Practice and Activity Book,* pp. 90–91.

Zum Schreiben

Objectives
Students will learn to use tone and word choice for effect.

- Do Motivating Activity, p. 155S, and read and discuss **Schreibtip,** p. 175.
- Have students do Activities A-C, p. 175. See the related suggestions, p.155S.

Anwendung

Objectives
Students will review and integrate all four skills and culture in preparation for the Chapter Test.

- Have students read **Im kreativen Rausch**, p. 176, and do Activity 1.
- Play the audio recording for Activity 2, p. 177 *(Audio CD 7),* and check for comprehension.
- Have students work in groups to do Activities 3 and 4, p. 177.
- Have students do **Kann ich's wirklich?,** p. 178, individually or with a partner.
- Have students review the vocabulary in **Wortschatz,** p. 179.
- Show **Videoclips: Werbung,** *Video Program (Videocassette 2).* See Activity Masters 1 and 2, *Video Guide,* pp. 33–34.

Assessment
- Chapter Test, *Testing Program,* pp. 155–160
- *Test Generator,* Chapter 7
- Speaking Test, *Testing Program,* p. 298
- *Alternative Assessment Guide,* pp. 22 and 36
- Suggested Project, *Annotated Teacher's Edition,* p. 155H

Resources
For correlated print and audiovisual materials, see *Annotated Teacher's Edition,* pp. 155A–155B.

STANDARDS FOR FOREIGN LANGUAGE LEARNING
Zum Lesen *Pupil's Edition:* (3.2) *Annotated Teacher's Edition:* (2.2; 3.2; 4.2; 5.2)
Zum Schreiben *Pupil's Edition:* (3.1) *Annotated Teacher's Edition:* (5.1)
Anwendung *Pupil's Edition:* (1.3; 5.1; 5.2) *Annotated Teacher's Edition:* (1.3; 3.2; 5.2)

Teacher's Name _____ Class _____ Date _____

KAPITEL 8
Weg mit den Vorurteilen!

Beginning the chapter (pp. 179A–183)

Activities in the shaded boxes enhance the basic lesson and are ideal for **block scheduling**.

Lesson Plans

Chapter Opener

- Do Motivating Activity, p. 179I.
- Have students look at photo #1, p. 180. See the related Teaching Suggestions, p. 179I.
- Have students look at photo #2, p. 181. See Thinking Critically: Analyzing, p. 179I.
- Ask students to complete the caption, **Die meisten von uns hätten nicht gedacht, dass es in Deutschland ... gibt,** with other observations.
- Have students look at photo #3, p. 181. See the related Teaching Suggestion, p. 179I.
- As students look at photo #3, p. 181, re-enter statements of comparison by asking them if they think Germans are more or less conscious of the environment (**umweltbewusst**) than Americans.
- Have students read the introduction at the top of p. 181 and briefly answer the questions posed in the paragraph.
- See Focusing on Outcomes, p. 179I.

Los geht's!

Objectives
Students will listen as German teenagers express their perceptions of the United States.

- Do Motivating Activity, p. 179J.
- Before presenting **Wie sehen uns die jungen Deutschen?**, pp. 182–183, you might choose to present **Wortschatz**, p. 184, which contains new vocabulary that students will encounter in **Los geht's!** See Presentation, p. 179K.
- Play the audio recording of **Wie sehen uns die jungen Deutschen?** *(Audio CD 8)*. Have students note as many of the Germans' reactions to the United States as they can.
- Replay the audio recording of **Wie sehen uns die jungen Deutschen?** Ask students to listen carefully to determine the lesson the German students draw from their experiences.
- Have students do Activity 1, p. 183. See Cooperative Learning, p. 179J.
- Have students reread **Wie sehen uns die jungen Deutschen?** and pick out the expressions the German students use to agree with one another, to differ with someone's opinion, and to emphasize a point.
- Ask students if they agree with the observations of the **Junge Deutsche, die in den Staaten waren,** pp. 182–183.
- See Closure, p. 179J.
- Have students do Activities 1 and 2, *Practice and Activity Book,* p. 92.

Resources
For correlated print and audiovisual materials, see *Annotated Teacher's Edition,* pp. 179A–179B.

STANDARDS FOR FOREIGN LANGUAGE LEARNING

Chapter Opener *Pupil's Edition:* (3.2; 4.2) *Annotated Teacher's Edition:* (2.1)
Los geht's! *Pupil's Edition:* (1.2) *Annotated Teacher's Edition:* (1.2; 5.2)

Teacher's Name _____ Class _____ Date _____

KAPITEL 8: Weg mit den Vorurteilen!

Erste Stufe (pp. 184–189)

Activities in the shaded boxes enhance the basic lesson and are ideal for **block scheduling**.

Lesson Plans

Objectives
Students will learn to express surprise, disappointment, and annoyance.

Motivate
See Teaching Suggestion, p. 179K.

Teach
1. Have students read **Meinung, Vorurteil oder Klischee?**, p. 184.
   Show Teaching Transparency 8-1, *Teaching Transparencies*, for work with stereotypes.
2. Have students work in groups to do Activity 4, p. 185.
3. Present **Wortschatz**, p. 184. See Presentation, p. 179K.
4. Play the audio recording for Activity 2, p. 184 *(Audio CD 8)*, and check for comprehension.
5. Have students work in groups to do Activity 3, p. 184.
6. Present **So sagt man das!** *(Expressing surprise, disappointment, and annoyance)*, p. 185.
   Have students do Activity 1, *Practice and Activity Book*, p. 93.
7. Play the audio recording for Activity 5, p. 185 *(Audio CD 8)*, and check for comprehension.
8. Have students pair off to do Activities 6 and 9, pp. 186, 187.
9. Present **Ein wenig Grammatik** *(The subordinating conjunction als)*, p. 187.
   Have students do Activity 4, *Grammar and Vocabulary Worksheets*, p. 66.
10. Have students do Activities 10 and 11, p. 187.
11. Present **Grammatik** *(Coordinating conjunctions)*, p. 188. See Presentation, p. 179L.
12. Have students write Activity 12, p. 188.
    Have students do Activities 4 and 5, *Practice and Activity Book*, pp. 94–95.
13. Have students work in groups to do Activity 15, p. 188.
14. Present **Landeskunde** and have students do activities 1-4, p. 189.
    Show the video clips **Asylanten in Frankfurt** and **Ausländer in Berlin**, *Video Program (Videocassette 2)*. See Activity Masters 1 and 2, *Video Guide*, pp. 37–38.

Additional Practice Options for Erste Stufe
- *Grammar and Vocabulary Worksheets*, pp. 64–67
- *Practice and Activity Book*, pp. 93–97
- Communicative Activity 8-1, *Activities for Communication*, pp. 29–30
- Situation 8-1 Interview and Role-playing, *Activities for Communication*, pp. 127–128
- Additional Listening Activities 8-1, 8-2, and 8-3, *Listening Activities*, pp. 63–64 *(Audio CD 8)*
- Realia 8-1, *Activities for Communication*, p. 86
- Teaching Transparency 8-1, *Teaching Transparencies*
- Additional Grammar Practice, *Pupil's Edition*, Activities 1-4, pp. R56–R57

Close
Close, p. 179M

Assess
Quiz 8-1A or 8-1B, *Testing Program*, pp. 169–172, and/or Performance Assessment, p. 179N

Resources
For correlated print and audiovisual materials, see *Annotated Teacher's Edition*, pp. 179A–179B.

STANDARDS FOR FOREIGN LANGUAGE LEARNING
Erste Stufe *Pupil's Edition:* (1.1; 1.3; 2.1; 4.1) *Annotated Teacher's Edition:* (1.1; 3.1; 4.2; 5.1)

Teacher's Name _____ Class _____ Date _____

KAPITEL 8

Weg mit den Vorurteilen!

Weiter geht's! (pp. 190–191)

Activities in the shaded boxes enhance the basic lesson and are ideal for **block scheduling**.

Lesson Plans

Weiter geht's!

Objectives
Students will be introduced to some perceptions young Americans have about Germany.

- Do Motivating Activity, p. 179N.
- Have students look at the illustration on p. 190 of the impressions of Germans held by young Americans who have never been in Germany.
- Have students do #1 of Activity 17, p. 191.
- Have students read the box of words at the bottom of p. 190. See Thinking Critically: Analyzing, p. 179N.
- Before students read the words in the box on p. 190, you might choose to present **Wortschatz**, p. 192, which includes new words that students will encounter in the box. See Presentation, p. 179O.
- To reinforce the vocabulary in the box on p. 190, have students categorize the words according to physical characteristics and character traits. Have them subdivide the character traits into positive traits and negative traits.
- For further practice with the vocabulary in the word box on p. 190, have students write sentences that suggest these words, without using them. Then hold a contest in which students read a sentence aloud and others try to guess the targeted word.
- Have students do #2 of Activity 17, p. 191.
- Play the audio recording (Audio CD 8) of the statements on p. 191 of the young Americans whose impressions of Germans changed following their visit to Germany.
- Have students do #3 of Activity 17, p. 191.
- Have students revise the illustration on p. 190 in light of the comments made on p. 191 by the young Americans who have visited Germany.
- Have students write a paragraph recommending changes in American society, based on the remarks of the young Americans on p. 191.
- See Closure, p. 179N.
- Have students do Activities 1 and 2, *Practice and Activity Book*, p. 98.

Resources
For correlated print and audiovisual materials, see *Annotated Teacher's Edition*, pp. 179A–179B.

STANDARDS FOR FOREIGN LANGUAGE LEARNING
Weiter geht's! *Pupil's Edition:* (2.2; 4.2) *Annotated Teacher's Edition:* (4.2)

48 Lesson Planner

Komm mit! Level 3

Copyright © by Holt, Rinehart and Winston. All rights reserved.

Teacher's Name _____ Class _____ Date _____

KAPITEL 8 — Weg mit den Vorurteilen!

Zweite Stufe (pp. 192–195)

Activities in the shaded boxes enhance the basic lesson and are ideal for **block scheduling**.

Lesson Plans

Objectives
Students will learn to express an assumption, make suggestions and recommendations, and give advice.

Motivate
See the related Teaching Suggestion, p. 179O.

Teach
1. Have students read **Der sympathische Deutsche,** p. 192. See the related Teaching Suggestion and Thinking Critically: Analyzing, p. 179O.
2. Present **Wortschatz,** p. 192. See Presentation, p. 179O.
   Have students do Activities 7 and 8, *Grammar and Vocabulary Worksheets*, p. 68.
3. Have students work in groups to do Activity 18, p. 192.
4. Play the audio recording for Activity 19, p. 192 *(Audio CD 8)*, and check for comprehension.
   Have students do Communicative Activity 8-3, *Activities for Communication*, pp. 31–32.
5. Have students work in groups to do Activities 20 and 21, p. 193.
6. Present **So sagt man das!** *(Expressing an assumption)*, p. 193. See Presentation, p. 179O.
7. Play the audio recording for Activity 22, p. 193 *(Audio CD 8)*, and check for comprehension.
   Have students do Activity 1, *Practice and Activity Book*, p. 99.
8. Have students pair off to do Activities 23 and 24, pp. 193, 194.
9. Present **Grammatik** *(Verbs with prefixes)*, p. 194. See Presentation, p. 179P.
   Have students do Activities 10-12, *Grammar and Vocabulary Worksheets*, pp. 70–71.
10. Present **So sagt man das!** *(Making suggestions and recommendations; giving advice)*, p. 195.
11. Have students do Activities 26 and 27, p. 195.
    Have students work in groups to do Activities 28 and 29, p. 195.
12. Have students write Activity 30, p. 195, in class or for homework.

Additional Practice Options for Zweite Stufe
- *Grammar and Vocabulary Worksheets*, pp. 68–72
- *Practice and Activity Book*, pp. 99–102
- Communicative Activities 8-2, 8-3, and 8-4, *Activities for Communication*, pp. 29–32
- Situation 8-2 Interview and Role-playing, *Activities for Communication*, pp. 127–128
- Additional Listening Activities 8-4, 8-5, and 8-6, *Listening Activities*, pp. 65–66 *(Audio CD 8)*
- Realia 8-2, *Activities for Communication*, p. 87
- Teaching Transparency 8-2, *Teaching Transparencies*
- Additional Grammar Practice, *Pupil's Edition*, Activities 5-8, pp. R57–R58

Close
Close, p. 179Q

Assess
Quiz 8-2A or 8-2B, *Testing Program*, pp. 173–176, and/or Performance Assessment, p. 179Q

Resources
For correlated print and audiovisual materials, see *Annotated Teacher's Edition*, pp. 179A–179B.

STANDARDS FOR FOREIGN LANGUAGE LEARNING
Zweite Stufe *Pupil's Edition:* (1.1; 1.3; 4.1) *Annotated Teacher's Edition:* (1.2)

Komm mit! Level 3

Copyright © by Holt, Rinehart and Winston. All rights reserved.

Teacher's Name _____ Class _____ Date _____

KAPITEL 8 — Weg mit den Vorurteilen!

Ending the chapter (pp. 196–203)

Activities in the shaded boxes enhance the basic lesson and are ideal for **block scheduling**.

Lesson Plans

Zum Lesen

Objectives
Students will learn to interpret rhetorical devices.

Prereading
- Do Motivating Activity, p. 179Q, and read and discuss **Lesetrick,** p. 196.

Reading
- Have students read the title and first paragraph up to „Wir sehen uns fast jeden Tag." and do Activities 1-3, pp. 196–197.
- Have students read the rest of the first paragraph and do Activity 4, p. 197.
- Have students finish reading the story and do Activities 5 10, pp. 197–198.

Postreading
- Have students do Activities 11 and 12, p. 198.
- For additional reading practice, see *Practice and Activity Book*, pp. 103–104.

Zum Schreiben

Objectives
Students will learn to select a point of view.

- Read and discuss **Schreibtip**, p. 199.
- Have students do Activities A-C, p. 199. See the related suggestions, p.179S.

Anwendung

Objectives
Students will review and integrate all four skills and culture in preparation for the Chapter Test.

- Play the audio recording for Activity 1, p. 200 *(Audio CD 8)*, and check for comprehension.
- Have students do Activities 2-4, p. 200.
- Have students do Activity 5, p. 200.
- Have students work in groups to do Activities 6-8, p. 201.
- Have students do **Kann ich's wirklich?,** p. 202, individually or with a partner.
- Have students review the vocabulary in **Wortschatz**, p. 203. See Game, p. 179T.
- Show **Videoclips: Werbung,** *Video Program (Videocassette 2)*. See Activity Master 2, *Video Guide*, p. 38.

Assessment
- Chapter Test, *Testing Program*, pp. 177–182
- *Test Generator*, Chapter 8
- Speaking Test, *Testing Program*, p. 298
- *Alternative Assessment Guide*, pp. 23 and 37
- Suggested Project, *Annotated Teacher's Edition*, p. 179H

Resources
For correlated print and audiovisual materials, see *Annotated Teacher's Edition*, pp. 179A–179B.

STANDARDS FOR FOREIGN LANGUAGE LEARNING
Zum Lesen *Pupil's Edition:* (3.2) *Annotated Teacher's Edition:* (2.1; 3.2)
Zum Schreiben *Pupil's Edition:* (3.1) *Annotated Teacher's Edition:* (1.3)
Anwendung *Pupil's Edition:* (5.1; 5.2) *Annotated Teacher's Edition:* (3.1)

Teacher's Name _____ Class _____ Date _____

KAPITEL 9
Aktiv für die Umwelt!

Beginning the chapter (pp. 203A–207)

Activities in the shaded boxes enhance the basic lesson and are ideal for **block scheduling**.

Lesson Plans

Chapter Opener

- Do Motivating Activity, p. 203I.
- Have students look at photo #1, p. 204. See Community Link, p. 203I.
- Have students use the caption of photo #1 as a model to create other sentences stating what good would result if we were to take an environmentally friendly action.
- Have students look at photo #2, p. 205. See Thinking Critically: Drawing Inferences, and the related Teaching Suggestion, p. 203I.
- Have students look at photo #3, p. 205. See the related Teaching Suggestions, p. 203I.
- Call students' attention to the objects in the margins of pp. 204–205. Ask them what messages these convey about ways to take care of the environment.
- See Focusing on Outcomes, p. 203I.

Los geht's!

Objectives
Students will listen to German teens talk about environmental concerns.

- Do Motivating Activity, p. 203I.
- Play the audio recording of **Für eine saubere Umwelt** *(Audio CD 9)*. Have students listen with their books closed. Tell them to note the danger(s) to the environment that each speaker identifies and at least one remedy each speaker proposes.
- Replay the audio recording of **Für eine saubere Umwelt.** Have students read along as they listen. Have them add to or correct their initial findings.
- For further practice with the vocabulary of **Für eine saubere Umwelt,** cite a danger to the environment in one sentence **(Die Industrie verpestet die Luft.)** and have students add another sentence to expand upon your quote **(Die Fabriken blasen Schadstoffe und Chemikalien in die Luft.).**
- Have students do Activities 1 and 2, p. 207.
- When students have compiled their lists of key words in Activity 2, p. 207, write the words in random order on a transparency and have students match those that refer to the same environmental problem.
- Have students work in groups to do Activity 3, p. 207.
- See Closure, p. 203J.
- Have students do Activity 1, *Practice and Activity Book,* p. 105.
- Show Teaching Transparency 9-1, *Teaching Transparencies,* a picture of a polluted planet Earth. Have students use the vocabulary of **Für eine saubere Umwelt** to describe the image.
- Show the interviews from **Landeskunde: Was tust du für die Umwelt?,** Level 1 *Video Program (Videocassette 3),* in which students tell what they do to protect the environment.

Resources
For correlated print and audiovisual materials, see *Annotated Teacher's Edition,* pp. 203A–203B.

STANDARDS FOR FOREIGN LANGUAGE LEARNING

Chapter Opener *Pupil's Edition:* (4.1; 4.2) *Annotated Teacher's Edition:* (2.1; 3.1; 4.2)
Los geht's! *Pupil's Edition:* (1.2; 1.3) *Annotated Teacher's Edition:* (1.2)

Teacher's Name _____ Class _____ Date _____

Aktiv für die Umwelt!

Erste Stufe (pp. 208–211)

Activities in the shaded boxes enhance the basic lesson and are ideal for **block scheduling**.

Lesson Plans

Objectives
Students will learn to express concern, make accusations, offer solutions, and make requests.

Motivate
See Game, p. 203J.

Teach
1. Present **Wortschatz**, p. 208. See Presentation, p. 203K.
   Have students do Activities 1-3, *Grammar and Vocabulary Worksheets*, pp. 73–74.
2. Present **So sagt man das!** *(Expressing concern)*, p. 208. See Presentation, p. 203K.
3. Play the audio recording for Activity 4, p. 208 *(Audio CD 9)*, and check for comprehension.
4. Have students pair off to do Activity 5, p. 209.
   Have students do Communicative Activity 9-1, *Activities for Communication*, pp. 33–34.
5. Present **So sagt man das!** *(Making accusations)*, p. 209. See Presentation, p. 203K.
6. Have students work in groups to do Activity 6, p. 209.
7. Have students pair off to do Activity 7, p. 210. See Group Work, p. 203K.
8. Present **So sagt man das!** *(Offering solutions)* and **Grammatik** *(Subjunctive forms of **können, müssen, dürfen, sollen,** and **sein**)*, p. 210. See Presentations, p. 203L.
   Have students do Activities 6 and 7, *Grammar and Vocabulary Worksheets*, pp. 75–76.
9. Play the audio recording for Activity 8, p. 210 *(Audio CD 9)*, and check for comprehension.
10. Have students work in groups to do Activity 9, p. 211.
11. Present **So sagt man das!** *(Making polite requests)*, p. 211. See Presentation, p. 203L.
    Have students do Activity 8, *Practice and Activity Book*, p. 109.
12. Have students pair off to do Activity 10, p. 211.
13. Have students write Activity 12, p. 211. See the related Teaching Suggestion, p. 203L.
    Show the video clip **Umweltprobleme**, *Video Program (Videocassette 2)*. See Teaching Suggestions, *Video Guide*, p. 40, and Activity Master 1, *Video Guide*, p. 41.

Additional Practice Options for Erste Stufe
- *Grammar and Vocabulary Worksheets*, pp. 73–76
- *Practice and Activity Book*, pp. 106–109
- Communicative Activities 9-1 and 9-2, *Activities for Communication*, pp. 33–34
- Situation 9-1 Interview and Role-playing, *Activities for Communication*, pp. 129–130
- Additional Listening Activities 9-1, 9-2, and 9-3, *Listening Activities*, pp. 71–72 *(Audio CD 9)*
- Realia 9-2, *Activities for Communication*, p. 92
- Teaching Transparency 9-1, *Teaching Transparencies*
- Additional Grammar Practice, *Pupil's Edition*, Activities 1-3, p. R59

Close
Close, p. 203L

Assess
Quiz 9-1A or 9-1B, *Testing Program*, pp. 191–194, and/or Performance Assessment, p. 203M

Resources
For correlated print and audiovisual materials, see *Annotated Teacher's Edition*, pp. 203A–203B.

STANDARDS FOR FOREIGN LANGUAGE LEARNING

Erste Stufe *Pupil's Edition:* (1.1; 1.3; 4.1) *Annotated Teacher's Edition:* (1.1; 4.1)

Teacher's Name _____ Class _____ Date _____

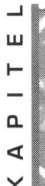

KAPITEL 9

Aktiv für die Umwelt!

Weiter geht's! (pp. 212–213)

Activities in the shaded boxes enhance the basic lesson and are ideal for **block scheduling**.

Lesson Plans

Weiter geht's!

Objectives
Students will listen to a discussion at a weekly meeting of an environmental club.

- Do Motivating Activity, p. 203M.
- Before presenting **Die Umwelt AG diskutiert: Umwelttips für Schüler,** pp. 212–213, you might choose to present **Wortschatz,** p. 214, which presents the new vocabulary that students will encounter in **Weiter geht's!** See Presentation, p. 203O.
- Have students read the introduction to **Die Umwelt AG diskutiert: Umwelttips für Schüler** and the three articles on p. 212. See Background Information and Teacher Note, p. 203M.
- Have students do Activity 13, p. 213. See Building on Previous Skills, p. 203M.
- Play the audio recording **Die Umwelt AG diskutiert: Umwelttips für Schüler** *(Audio CD 9)* as students listen with their books closed. Ask them to give the gist of each speaker's remarks.
- Replay the audio recording of **Die Umwelt AG diskutiert: Umwelttips für Schüler** as students read along in their books. Have them modify their first impressions.
- Have students do Activity 15, p. 213. See the related Teaching Suggestion, p. 203N.
- For further challenge, have students play the role of **Umweltmuffel** and compose a response to each of the German students that presents an opposing viewpoint.
- Have students do Activity 14, p. 213.
- To review previously learned material, ask students to write sentences using the indicative instead of the subjunctive, in order to describe the present practices in the **Gymnasium** that these students would like to change.
- See Closure, p. 203N.
- Have students do Activities 1 and 2, *Practice and Activity Book,* p.110.

Resources
For correlated print and audiovisual materials, see *Annotated Teacher's Edition,* pp. 203A–203B.

STANDARDS FOR FOREIGN LANGUAGE LEARNING
Weiter geht's! *Pupil's Edition:* (2.2; 4.2) *Annotated Teacher's Edition:* (2.1; 2.2)

Komm mit! Level 3 Lesson Planner **53**
Copyright © by Holt, Rinehart and Winston. All rights reserved.

Teacher's Name _____ Class _____ Date _____

KAPITEL 9 — Aktiv für die Umwelt!

Zweite Stufe (pp. 214–219)

Activities in the shaded boxes enhance the basic lesson and are ideal for **block scheduling**.

Lesson Plans

Objectives
Students will learn to say what is being done about a problem, offer solutions, and hypothesize.

Motivate
See Game, p. 203N.

Teach
1. Present **Wortschatz,** p. 214. See Presentation, p. 203O.
   Have students do Activities 9-11, *Grammar and Vocabulary Worksheets,* pp. 77–78.
2. Have students pair off to do Activity 16, p. 214. See For Additional Practice, p. 203O.
3. Play the audio recording for Activity 17, p. 215 *(Audio CD 9),* and check for comprehension.
4. Present **Grammatik** *(The passive voice, present tense),* p. 215. See Presentation, p. 203O.
5. Present **So sagt man das!** *(Saying what is being done about a problem),* p. 215. See Presentation, p. 203O.
   Have students do Activities 1 and 2, *Practice and Activity Book,* p. 111.
6. Play the audio recording for Activity 19, p. 215 *(Audio CD 9),* and check for comprehension.
7. Have students work in groups to do Activity 20, p. 216.
8. Present **So sagt man das!** *(Offering solutions)* and **Ein wenig Grammatik** *(The passive voice with modals),* p. 216. See Presentation, p. 203O.
   Have students do Activity 14, *Grammar and Vocabulary Worksheets,* p. 79.
9. Have students pair off to do Activity 22, p. 216.
10. Present **So sagt man das!** *(Hypothesizing)* and **Grammatik** *(Conditional sentences),* p. 217. See Presentations, p. 203O.
11. Play the audio recording for Activity 23, p. 218 *(Audio CD 9),* and check for comprehension.
12. Have students work in groups to do Activities 24 and 25, p. 218.
    Show the video clip **Die Umwelt in der Ex-DDR,** *Video Program (Videocassette 2).* See Teaching Suggestions, *Video Guide,* p. 40, and Activity Master 1, *Video Guide,* p. 41.
13. Have students do Activities 26 and 27, p. 218.
14. Present **Landeskunde** and have students do questions 1-4, p. 219.

Additional Practice Options for Zweite Stufe
- *Grammar and Vocabulary Worksheets,* pp. 77–81
- *Practice and Activity Book,* pp. 111–115
- Communicative Activity 9-4, *Activities for Communication,* pp. 35–36
- Situation 9-2 Interview and Role-playing, *Activities for Communication,* pp. 129–130
- Additional Listening Activities 9-4, 9-5, and 9-6, *Listening Activities,* pp. 72–74 *(Audio CD 9)*
- Realia 9-1 and 9-2, *Activities for Communication,* pp. 91–92
- Teaching Transparency 9-2, *Teaching Transparencies*
- Additional Grammar Practice, *Pupil's Edition,* Activities 4-7, pp. R60–R61

Close
Close, p. 203P

Assess
Quiz 9-2A or 9-2B, *Testing Program,* pp. 195–198, and/or Performance Assessment, p. 203P

Resources
For correlated print and audiovisual materials, see *Annotated Teacher's Edition,* pp. 203A–203B.

STANDARDS FOR FOREIGN LANGUAGE LEARNING
Zweite Stufe *Pupil's Edition:* (1.1; 2.1; 4.1) *Annotated Teacher's Edition:* (1.1; 1.2)

Teacher's Name _____ Class _____ Date _____

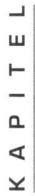

KAPITEL 9

Aktiv für die Umwelt!

Ending the chapter (pp. 220–227)
Activities in the shaded boxes enhance the basic lesson and are ideal for **block scheduling**.

Lesson Plans

Zum Lesen

Objectives
Students will learn to interpret statistics.

Prereading
- Do Motivating Activity, p. 203Q, and read and discuss **Lesetrick,** p. 220.
- Have students do Activity 1, p. 220. See the related Teaching Suggestion, p. 203Q.

Reading
- Have students do Activities 2-8, pp. 220-222.

Postreading
- Have students do Activities 9 and 10, p. 222. See the related Teaching Suggestion, p. 203Q.
- For additional reading practice, see *Practice and Activity Book,* pp. 116-117.

Zum Schreiben

Objectives
Students will learn to analyze their audience.

- Do Motivating Activity, p. 203R, and read and discuss **Schreibtip,** p. 223.
- Have students do Activities A-C, p. 223. See the related suggestions, pp.203R-203S.

Anwendung

Objectives
Students will review and integrate all four skills and culture in preparation for the Chapter Test.

- Have students read **Das saubere Klassenzimmer** in Activity 1, p. 224.
- Play the audio recording for Activity 2, p. 224 *(Audio CD 9),* and check for comprehension.
- Have students work in groups to do Activity 4, p. 225.
- Have students do Activity 6, p. 225. See the related Teaching Suggestion, p. 203T.
- Have students do **Kann ich's wirklich?**, p. 226, individually or with a partner.
- Have students review the vocabulary in **Wortschatz,** p. 227.
- Show **Videoclips: Werbung,** *Video Program (Videocassette 2).* See Activity Master 2, *Video Guide,* p. 42.

Assessment
- Chapter Test, *Testing Program,* pp. 199-204
- *Test Generator,* Chapter 9
- Speaking Test, *Testing Program,* p. 299
- *Alternative Assessment Guide,* pp. 24 and 38
- Suggested Project, *Annotated Teacher's Edition,* p. 203H

Resources
For correlated print and audiovisual materials, see *Annotated Teacher's Edition,* pp. 203A-203B.

STANDARDS FOR FOREIGN LANGUAGE LEARNING
Zum Lesen *Pupil's Edition:* (3.2) *Annotated Teacher's Edition:* (3.2)
Zum Schreiben *Pupil's Edition:* (3.1) *Annotated Teacher's Edition:* (3.1; 5.2)
Anwendung *Pupil's Edition:* (5.1; 5.2) *Annotated Teacher's Edition:* (1.1; 1.3; 3.1)

Komm mit! Level 3   Lesson Planner **55**

Teacher's Name _____ Class _____ Date _____

KAPITEL 10 — Die Kunst zu leben

Beginning the chapter (pp. 227A–235)

Activities in the shaded boxes enhance the basic lesson and are ideal for **block scheduling**.

Lesson Plans

Location Opener

Objectives
Students will learn about famous people, historical events, and places in Dresden.

- Have students do the Pre-viewing Activity, *Video Guide*, p. 44.
- Show **Komm mit nach Dresden!**, *Video Program* (Videocassette 2).
- Have students do the Viewing Activity, *Video Guide*, p. 44.
- See the Post-viewing Suggestions, *Video Guide*, p. 43.

Chapter Opener

- Have students look at photo #1, p. 232. See Culture Note, p. 231I.
- Do Motivating Activity, p. 231I.
- Have students look at photo #2, p. 233. See Thinking Critically: Drawing Inferences and Drama Connection, p. 231I.
- As students look at photo #2, p. 233, ask them **Wo sind diese Leute? Was sehen sie sich an?**
- Have students look at photo #3, p. 233. See For Individual Needs: Visual Learners and Teaching Suggestion, p. 231I.
- See Focusing on Outcomes, p. 231I.

Los geht's!

Objectives
Students will listen to four German teens talk about their cultural interests.

- Do Motivating Activity, p. 231J.
- Play the segment of the audio recording of **Was tun für die Kultur?** *(Audio CD 10)* that includes the interviewer's first question and the students' answers. Read aloud true/false statements that you have created about the first segment of the recording.
- Play the next segment of the audio recording of **Was tun für die Kultur?** that includes the interviewer's second question about museums and art expositions and the students' answers. Ask students what the speakers have to say about student attendance at museums, opera, theater, and concerts.
- Play the remainder of the audio recording of **Was tun für die Kultur?**
- Have students do Activities 1–3, p. 235.
- See Closure, p. 231J.
- Have students do Activities 1 and 2, *Practice and Activity Book*, p. 118.

Resources
For correlated print and audiovisual materials, see Annotated Teacher's Edition, pp. 231A–231B.

STANDARDS FOR FOREIGN LANGUAGE LEARNING

Location Opener *Pupil's Edition:* (3.1; 4.2) *Annotated Teacher's Edition:* (2.2; 3.1)
Chapter Opener *Pupil's Edition:* (4.1; 4.2) *Annotated Teacher's Edition:* (2.1; 2.2; 3.1)
Los geht's! *Pupil's Edition:* (1.2; 1.3) *Annotated Teacher's Edition:* (1.1; 4.2; 5.2)

Teacher's Name _____ Class _____ Date _____

KAPITEL 10

Die Kunst zu leben

Erste Stufe (pp. 236–239)

Activities in the shaded boxes enhance the basic lesson and are ideal for **block scheduling**.

Lesson Plans

Objectives
Students will learn to express preference, envy, and admiration.

Motivate
See Game, p. 231K.

Teach
1. Present **Wortschatz**, p. 236. See Presentation and Teacher Note, p. 231K.
   Have students do Activities 1–3, *Grammar and Vocabulary Worksheets*, p. 82.
2. Present **So sagt man das!** *(Expressing preference, given certain possibilities)*, p. 236. See Presentation, p. 231K.
3. Play the audio recording for Activity 4, p. 236 *(Audio CD 10)*, and check for comprehension.
4. Have students pair off to do Activity 5, p. 237.
   Have students do Communicative Activity 10-1, *Activities for Communication*, pp. 37–38.
5. Have students pair off to do Activities 6 and 7, p. 237.
   Have students do Activity 1, *Practice and Activity Book*, p. 119.
7. Present **So sagt man das!** *(Expressing envy and admiration)*, p. 237. See Presentation, p. 231L.
   Have students do Activity 5, *Grammar and Vocabulary Worksheets*, p. 84.
8. Have students pair off to do Activity 8, p. 238.
9. Present **Grammatik** *(Prepositions with the genitive case)*, p. 238. See Presentation, p. 231L.
10. Have students write Activity 9, p. 238.
    Have students do Activities 2 and 3, *Practice and Activity Book*, pp. 119–120.
11. Have students pair off to do Activity 10, p. 238.
13. Have students work in groups to do Activities 13 and 14, p. 239.
15. Have students write Activity 15, p. 239, in class or for homework.

Additional Practice Options for Erste Stufe
- *Grammar and Vocabulary Worksheets*, pp. 82–85
- *Practice and Activity Book*, pp. 119–122
- Communicative Activities 10-1 and 10-2, *Activities for Communication*, pp. 37–38
- Situation 10-1 Interview and Role-playing, *Activities for Communication*, pp. 131–132
- Additional Listening Activities 10-1, 10-2, and 10-3, *Listening Activities*, pp. 79–80 *(Audio CD 10)*
- Realia 10-1, *Activities for Communication*, p. 96
- Teaching Transparency 10-1, *Teaching Transparencies*
- Additional Grammar Practice, *Pupil's Edition*, Activities 1–2, p. R61

Close
Close, p. 231M

Assess
Quiz 10-1A or 10-1B, *Testing Program*, pp. 213–216, and/or Performance Assessment, p. 231M

Resources
For correlated print and audiovisual materials, see *Annotated Teacher's Edition*, pp. 231A–231B.

STANDARDS FOR FOREIGN LANGUAGE LEARNING
Erste Stufe *Pupil's Edition:* (1.1; 1.3; 4.1) *Annotated Teacher's Edition:* (1.1; 2.2)

Komm mit! Level 3   Lesson Planner **57**

Copyright © by Holt, Rinehart and Winston. All rights reserved.

Teacher's Name _____ Class _____ Date _____

KAPITEL 10
Die Kunst zu leben

Weiter geht's! (pp. 240–241)

Activities in the shaded boxes enhance the basic lesson and are ideal for **block scheduling**.

Lesson Plans

Weiter geht's!

Objectives
Students will listen to and read an article about a class trip to the ballet.

- Do Motivating Activity, p. 231M.
- Before presenting **Ein kulturelles Erlebnis für die Schüler,** pp. 240–241, you might choose to present **Wortschatz,** p. 242, which includes new vocabulary that students will encounter in **Weiter geht's!** See Presentation, p. 231O.
- Have students read the introduction to **Ein kulturelles Erlebnis für die Schüler.** See both Teaching Suggestions, p. 231M.
- Play the audio recording of **Ein kulturelles Erlebnis für die Schüler** (Audio CD 10) through once as students listen with their books closed. Have them share whatever they understood.
- Replay the audio recording of the first paragraph of **Ein kulturelles Erlebnis für die Schüler,** which recounts the preparations made by the teacher for the class trip to the ballet. Ask students to tell what the teacher did and describe the reactions of the writer and of the boys in the class.
- Replay the audio recording of the second paragraph of **Ein kulturelles Erlebnis für die Schüler,** which concerns the arrival at the theater. Have students describe the mood of the writer, the seating of the students, the impression of the theater, and the orchestra's preparations.
- Replay the audio recording of the third paragraph of **Ein kulturelles Erlebnis für die Schüler,** in which the writer highlights the anticipation of the start of the ballet. Ask students to describe the indications that the ballet was about to begin.
- Replay the audio recording of the fourth paragraph of **Ein kulturelles Erlebnis für die Schüler,** which focuses on the ballet from beginning to end. Ask students to tell what they learned of the story of the ballet and to describe the audience's reaction at the end.
- Replay the audio recording of the fifth paragraph of **Ein kulturelles Erlebnis für die Schüler,** which describes the next day at school. Ask students to describe the two reactions of the class to their experience.
- Have students do questions 1-4 of Activity 16, p. 241.
- Once students have done #4 of Activity 16, p. 241, and written the list of adjectives they found in the article, have them close their books. Write on the board in random order the nouns that these adjectives described in the text. Have students match the nouns with their corresponding adjectives.
- See Closure, p. 231N.
- Have students do Activities 1 and 2, *Practice and Activity Book*, p.123.
- Show the interviews from **Landeskunde: Für welche kulturellen Veranstaltungen interessierst du dich?,** Level 2 *Video Program (Videocassette 4).*

Resources
For correlated print and audiovisual materials, see *Annotated Teacher's Edition,* pp. 231A–231B.

STANDARDS FOR FOREIGN LANGUAGE LEARNING
Weiter geht's! *Pupil's Edition:* (2.2; 4.2) *Annotated Teacher's Edition:* (1.2; 2.2)

Teacher's Name _____ Class _____ Date _____

KAPITEL 10 — Die Kunst zu leben

Zweite Stufe (pp. 242–247)

Activities in the shaded boxes enhance the basic lesson and are ideal for **block scheduling**.

Lesson Plans

Objectives
Students will learn to express happiness and sadness and say that something is or was being done.

Motivate
- See Teaching Suggestion, p. 231O.

Teach
1. Present **Wortschatz,** p. 242. See Presentation, p. 231O.
   Have students do Activities 7 and 8, *Grammar and Vocabulary Worksheets,* p. 86.
2. Present **So sagt man das!** *(Expressing happiness and sadness),* p. 242. See Presentation, p. 231O.
3. Play the audio recording for Activity 17, p. 243 *(Audio CD 10),* and check for comprehension.
4. Have students pair off to do Activity 18, p. 243.
5. Present **Ein wenig Grammatik** *(The da- and wo-compounds),* p. 243. See Presentation, p. 231O.
   Have students do Activity 7, *Practice and Activity Book,* p. 127.
8. Have students write Activities 21 and 22, p. 244.
10. Present **So sagt man das!** *(Saying that something is or was being done),* p. 244.
11. Play the audio recording for Activity 23, p. 244 *(Audio CD 10),* and check for comprehension.
    Have students do Communicative Activity 10-4, *Activities for Communication,* pp. 39–40.
13. Present **Grammatik** *(The passive voice),* p. 245. See Presentation, p. 231P.
14. Have students write Activity 25, p. 246.
15. Have students pair off to do Activities 26 and 28, p. 246.
    See Reteaching: Passive Voice, p. 231P.
    Have students work in groups to do Activity 27, p. 246.
17. Present **Landeskunde** and have students do Activities A and B, p. 247.
    Show the video clip **Geld für Kultur,** *Video Program (Videocassette 2).* See Activity Master 1, *Video Guide,* p. 47.

Additional Practice Options for Zweite Stufe
- *Grammar and Vocabulary Worksheets,* pp. 86–90
- *Practice and Activity Book,* pp. 124–128
- Communicative Activities 10-3 and 10-4, *Activities for Communication,* pp. 39–40
- Situation 10-2 Interview and Role-playing, *Activities for Communication,* pp. 131–132
- Additional Listening Activities 10-4, 10-5, and 10-6, *Listening Activities,* pp. 81–82 *(Audio CD 10)*
- Realia 10-2 and 10-3, *Activities for Communication,* pp. 97–98
- *Teaching Transparency 10-2, Teaching Transparencies*
- Additional Grammar Practice, *Pupil's Edition,* Activities 3–8, pp. R62–R63

Close
Close, p. 231Q

Assess
Quiz 10-2A or 10-2B, *Testing Program,* pp. 217–220, and/or Performance Assessment, p. 231Q

Resources
For correlated print and audiovisual materials, see *Annotated Teacher's Edition,* pp. 231A–231B.

STANDARDS FOR FOREIGN LANGUAGE LEARNING

Zweite Stufe *Pupil's Edition:* (1.1; 1.3; 2.1; 4.1) *Annotated Teacher's Edition:* (3.2)

Teacher's Name _____ Class _____ Date _____

KAPITEL 10 — Die Kunst zu leben

Ending the chapter (pp. 248–255)

Activities in the shaded boxes enhance the basic lesson and are ideal for **block scheduling**.

Lesson Plans

Zum Lesen

Objectives
Students will learn to read for comprehension.

Prereading
- Do Motivating Activity, p. 231R, and read and discuss **Lesetrick**, p. 248.
- Have students do Activity 1, p. 248.

Reading
- Have students read the first paragraph and do Activities 2–4, pp. 248–249.
- Have students read paragraphs 2–6 and do Activity 5, pp. 249–250.
- Have students finish reading the story and do Activities 6–11, p. 250.

Postreading
- Have students do Activity 12, p. 250.
- For additional reading practice, see *Practice and Activity Book*, pp. 129–130.

Zum Schreiben

Objectives
Students will learn to use figurative language and sound devices.

- Do Motivating Activity, p. 231S, and read and discuss **Schreibtip**, p. 251.
- Have students do Activities A–C, p. 251. See the related suggestions, p. 231S.

Anwendung

Objectives
Students will review and integrate all four skills and culture in preparation for the Chapter Test.

- Play the audio recording for Activity 1, p. 252 *(Audio CD 10)*, and check for comprehension.
- Have students do Activities 2 and 3, p. 252. See Music Connection, p. 231T.
- Have students do Activity 6 and play the game in Activity 7, p. 253.
- Have students do **Kann ich's wirklich?**, p. 254, individually or with a partner.
- Have students review the vocabulary in **Wortschatz**, p. 255. See Game, p. 231T.
- Show **Videoclips: Werbung**, *Video Program (Videocassette 2)*. See Teaching Suggestions, *Video Guide*, p. 46, and Activity Master 2, *Video Guide*, p. 48.

Assessment
- Chapter Test, *Testing Program*, pp. 221–226
- *Test Generator*, Chapter 10
- Speaking Test, *Testing Program*, p. 299
- *Alternative Assessment Guide*, pp. 25 and 39
- Suggested Project, *Annotated Teacher's Edition*, p. 231H

Resources
For correlated print and audiovisual materials, see *Annotated Teacher's Edition*, pp. 231A–231B.

STANDARDS FOR FOREIGN LANGUAGE LEARNING
Zum Lesen *Pupil's Edition:* (3.2) *Annotated Teacher's Edition:* (5.2)
Zum Schreiben *Pupil's Edition:* (3.1) *Annotated Teacher's Edition:* (1.1; 3.1; 5.1)
Anwendung *Pupil's Edition:* (5.1; 5.2) *Annotated Teacher's Edition:* (1.3)

Teacher's Name _____ Class _____ Date _____

KAPITEL 11 — Deine Welt ist deine Sache!

Beginning the chapter (pp. 255A–259)

Activities in the shaded boxes enhance the basic lesson and are ideal for **block scheduling**.

Lesson Plans

Chapter Opener

- Do Motivating Activity, p. 255I.
- Have students look at photo #1, p. 256. See the related Background Information and Thinking Critically: Drawing Inferences, p. 255I.
- Have students look at photo #2, p. 257. See the related Thinking Critically: Analyzing, Culture Note, and Building on Previous Skills, p. 255I.
- Have students look at photo #3, p. 257. See the related Teaching Suggestion, p. 255I.
- Call attention to the document at the bottom right of p. 257. Ask students what they think it is.
- See Focusing on Outcomes, p. 255I.

Los geht's!

Objectives
Students will listen to German students talk about what they plan to do after graduation.

- Do Motivating Activity, p. 255J.
- Before presenting **Was kommt nach der Schule?**, pp. 258–259, you might choose to present **Wortschatz**, p. 260, which includes new vocabulary that students will encounter in **Los geht's!** See Presentation, p. 255K.
- Have students read the introductory paragraph of **Was kommt nach der Schule?**, p. 258. See Building on Previous Skills, p. 255J.
- Play the audio recording of each teenager's remarks in **Was kommt nach der Schule?** *(Audio CD 11)* as students listen with their books closed. Pause after each speaker finishes and ask students for a short summary of what the German teen said.
- Replay the audio recording of the four interviews in **Was kommt nach der Schule?** Have students read along as they listen and add to or correct their first impressions.
- Have students do Activity 1, p. 259. See the related Teaching Suggestion and For Individual Needs: A Slower Pace, p. 255J.
- Have students read the survey results on p. 259.
- Have students do Activity 2, p. 259. See the related For Individual Needs: A Slower Pace, Thinking Critically: Analyzing, and Teaching Suggestion, p. 255J.
- Have students do Activity 3, p. 259. See the related Teaching Suggestion, p. 255J.
- See Closure, p. 255J.
- Have students do Activities 1 and 2, *Practice and Activity Book*, p. 131.
- Show the video clip **Azubis in Dresden**, *Video Program (Videocassette 2)*, in which three young apprentices in technical fields describe what they are learning and why they chose an apprenticeship. See Teaching Suggestions, *Video Guide*, p. 50, and Activity Master 2, *Video Guide*, p. 52.

Resources
For correlated print and audiovisual materials, see *Annotated Teacher's Edition*, pp. 255A–255B.

STANDARDS FOR FOREIGN LANGUAGE LEARNING

Chapter Opener *Pupil's Edition:* (3.2; 4.2) *Annotated Teacher's Edition:* (2.1)
Los geht's! *Pupil's Edition:* (1.2; 1.3) *Annotated Teacher's Edition:* (1.2)

Komm mit! Level 3   Lesson Planner **61**

Teacher's Name _____ Class _____ Date _____

KAPITEL 11 — Deine Welt ist deine Sache!

Erste Stufe (pp. 260–265)

Activities in the shaded boxes enhance the basic lesson and are ideal for **block scheduling**.

Lesson Plans

Objectives
Students will learn to express determination or indecision and talk about whether something is or is not important.

Motivate
See Game, p. 255K.

Teach
1. Present **Wortschatz,** p. 260. See Presentation, p. 255K.
   Have students do Activities 1–3, *Grammar and Vocabulary Worksheets,* pp. 91–92.
2. Present **So sagt man das!** *(Expressing determination or indecision)*, p. 260.
3. Play the audio recording for Activity 4, p. 261 *(Audio CD 11)*, and check for comprehension.
4. Have students pair off to do Activities 6 and 8, pp. 261, 262.
5. Present **Ein wenig Landeskunde,** p. 262. See Presentation, p. 255L.
   Show the video clip **Neue Lehrpläne,** *Video Program (Videocassette 2).* See Activity Master 1, *Video Guide,* p. 51.
6. Have students write Activity 9, p. 262, in class or for homework.
7. Present **So sagt man das!** *(Talking about whether something is important or not important)*, p. 263. See Presentation, p. 255L.
8. Play the audio recording for Activity 12, p. 263 *(Audio CD 11)*, and check for comprehension.
   Have students do Activity 6, *Grammar and Vocabulary Worksheets,* p. 94.
9. Present **Ein wenig Grammaik,** p. 263.
   Have students do Activity 5, *Practice and Activity Book,* p. 134.
10. Have students work in groups to do Activity 13, p. 263.
11. Present **Wortschatz,** p. 264. See Presentation, p. 255M.
12. Have students work in groups to do Activity 15, p. 264.
    Have students do Communicative Activity 11-3, *Activities for Communication,* pp. 43–44.
13. Have students write Activity 16, p. 264, in class or for homework.
14. Present **Landeskunde** and have students do Activities A and B, p. 265.

Additional Practice Options for Erste Stufe
- *Grammar and Vocabulary Worksheets,* pp. 91–94
- *Practice and Activity Book,* pp. 132–136
- Communicative Activities 11-1, 11-2, and 11-3, *Activities for Communication,* pp. 41–44
- Situation 11-1 Interview and Role-playing, *Activities for Communication,* pp. 133–134
- Additional Listening Activities 11-1, 11-2, and 11-3, *Listening Activities,* pp. 87–88 *(Audio CD 11)*
- Realia 11-1, *Activities for Communication,* p. 101
- *Teaching Transparency 11-1, Teaching Transparencies*
- Additional Grammar Practice, *Pupil's Edition,* Activities 1–3, pp. R63–R64

Close
Close, p. 255N.

Assess
Quiz 11-1A or 11-1B, *Testing Program,* pp. 235–238, and/or Performance Assessment, p. 255N

Resources
For correlated print and audiovisual materials, see *Annotated Teacher's Edition,* pp. 255A–255B.

STANDARDS FOR FOREIGN LANGUAGE LEARNING
Erste Stufe *Pupil's Edition:* (1.1; 2.1; 2.2; 4.1) *Annotated Teacher's Edition:* (1.1)

Teacher's Name _____ Class _____ Date _____

KAPITEL 11 — Deine Welt ist deine Sache!

Weiter geht's! (pp. 266–267)

Activities in the shaded boxes enhance the basic lesson and are ideal for **block scheduling**.

Lesson Plans

Weiter geht's!

Objectives
Students will listen to German teenagers talk about their future.

- Do Motivating Activity, p. 255N.
- Before presenting **Wenn ich mal dreißig bin, ...**, pp. 266–267, you might choose to present **Wortschatz**, p. 268, which includes new vocabulary that students will encounter in **Weiter geht's!** See Presentation, p. 255O.
- Play the audio recording of each teenager's interview in **Wenn ich mal dreißig bin, ...** *(Audio CD 11)*, as students listen with their books closed. Pause the recording after each teen finishes speaking and ask students to summarize what each one said.
- Replay the audio recording of **Wenn ich mal dreißig bin, ...** in its entirety as students read along in their books. Ask them to compare the teenagers' outlooks on the future.
- Have students read aloud any remarks made by these teenagers that they agree with or that reflect their own situation.
- Have students describe the photos on p. 267. Ask them to match the photos with the interviews and explain their choices.
- Have students write Activity 17, p. 267. See the related Teaching Suggestion, p. 255N.
- After students have completed Activity 17, p. 267, play a game in which two teams choose and read aloud statements at random from the five interviews and take turns challenging each other to identify the speakers.
- Have students work in groups to do Activity 18, p. 267. See Thinking Critically: Comparing and Contrasting, p. 255N.
- When students have finished Activity 18, p. 267, ask them to write a paragraph about themselves. They should model it on the interviews and might even select sentences from the interviews to incorporate into their own paragraph.
- Assign each interview to one or more groups. Tell students to rewrite the interview in the third person.
- See Closure, p. 255N.
- Have students do Activities 1 and 2, *Practice and Activity Book*, p.137.

Resources
For correlated print and audiovisual materials, see *Annotated Teacher's Edition*, pp. 255A–255B.

STANDARDS FOR FOREIGN LANGUAGE LEARNING

Weiter geht's! *Pupil's Edition:* (2.2; 4.2) *Annotated Teacher's Edition:* (4.2)

Komm mit! Level 3 — Lesson Planner

Teacher's Name _____ Class _____ Date _____

KAPITEL 11 — Deine Welt ist deine Sache!

Zweite Stufe (pp. 268–271)

Activities in the shaded boxes enhance the basic lesson and are ideal for **block scheduling**.

Lesson Plans

Objectives
Students will learn to express wishes, express certainty, refuse or accept with certainty, talk about goals for the future, and express relief.

Motivate
- See the related Teaching Suggestion, p. 255O.

Teach
1. Present **Wortschatz,** p. 268. See Presentation, p. 255O.
   Have students do Activities 8–11, *Grammar and Vocabulary Worksheets,* pp. 95–96.
2. Have students read the survey results in **Wie sieht die Jugend ihre Zukunft?** and do Activity 19, p. 269.
3. Present **So sagt man das!** *(Expressing wishes),* p. 269. See Presentation, p. 255O.
4. Play the audio recording for Activity 20, p. 269 *(Audio CD 11),* and check for comprehension.
5. Have students pair off to do Activity 21, p. 269.
6. Present **So sagt man das!** *(Expressing certainty . . .),* p. 269. See Presentation, p. 255P.
7. Have students do Activities 23 and 24, p. 270.
8. Present **Ein wenig Grammatik** *(Expressing future time),* p. 270. See Presentation, p. 255P.
   Have students do Activity 1, *Practice and Activity Book,* p. 138.
9. Have students work in groups to do Activity 25, p. 270.
10. Present **So sagt man das!** *(Talking about goals for the future),* p. 270, and **Grammatik** *(The perfect infinitive with modals and* **werden***),* p. 271.
11. Play the audio recording for Activity 26, p. 270 *(Audio CD 11),* and check for comprehension.
12. Have students work in groups to do Activity 27, p. 271.
13. Have students write Activity 28, p. 271, in class or for homework.
14. Present **So sagt man das!** *(Expressing relief),* p. 271. See Presentation, p. 255Q.
    Have students do Activities 6 and 7, *Practice and Activity Book,* pp. 140–141.
15. Have students work in groups to do Activity 29, p. 271.
16. Have students write Activity 30, p. 271, in class or for homework.

Additional Practice Options for Zweite Stufe
- *Grammar and Vocabulary Worksheets,* pp. 95–99
- *Practice and Activity Book,* pp. 138–141
- Communicative Activity 11-4, *Activities for Communication,* pp. 43–44
- Situation 11-2 Interview and Role-playing, *Activities for Communication,* pp. 133–134
- Additional Listening Activities 11-4, 11-5, and 11-6, *Listening Activities,* pp. 88–90 *(Audio CD 11)*
- Realia 11-2 and 11-3, *Activities for Communication,* pp. 102–103
- *Teaching Transparency 11-2, Teaching Transparencies*
- Additional Grammar Practice, *Pupil's Edition,* Activities 4–7, pp. R65–R66

Close
Close, p. 255Q

Assess
Quiz 11-2A or 11-2B, *Testing Program,* pp. 239–242, and/or Performance Assessment, p. 255Q

Resources
For correlated print and audiovisual materials, see *Annotated Teacher's Edition,* pp. 255A–255B.

STANDARDS FOR FOREIGN LANGUAGE LEARNING
Zweite Stufe *Pupil's Edition:* (1.1; 1.3; 4.1) *Annotated Teacher's Edition:* (1.1; 3.1; 5.2)

Teacher's Name _____ Class _____ Date _____

KAPITEL 11

Deine Welt ist deine Sache!

Ending the chapter (pp. 272–279)

Activities in the shaded boxes enhance the basic lesson and are ideal for **block scheduling**.

Lesson Plans

Zum Lesen

Objectives
Students will learn to interpret symbols.

Prereading
- Do Motivating Activity, p. 255R, and read and discuss **Lesetrick,** p. 272.
- Have students do Activities 1 and 2, p. 272.

Reading
- Have students do Activities 3–9, pp. 272–274. See the related Teacher Notes, p. 255R.

Postreading
- Have students do Activity 10, p. 274.
- For additional reading practice, see *Practice and Activity Book,* pp. 142–143.

Zum Schreiben

Objectives
Students will learn to write drafts and revise.

- Do Motivating Activity, p. 255S, and read and discuss **Schreibtip,** p. 275.
- Have students do Activities A–C, p. 275. See the related suggestions, p. 255S.

Anwendung

Objectives
Students will review and integrate all four skills and culture in preparation for the Chapter Test.

- Play the audio recording for Activity 1, p. 276 *(Audio CD 11),* and check for comprehension.
- Have students do Activities 2 and 3, p. 276.
- Have students work in groups to do Activity 4, p. 276.
- Have students do Activities 5 and 6, pp. 276–277.
- Have students do Activity 7, p. 277.
- Have students do **Kann ich's wirklich?,** p. 278, individually or with a partner.
- Have students review the vocabulary in **Wortschatz,** p. 279.
- Show **Videoclips: Werbung,** *Video Program (Videocassette 2).* See Activity Master 2, *Video Guide,* p. 52.

Assessment
- Chapter Test, *Testing Program,* pp. 243–248
- *Test Generator,* Chapter 11
- Speaking Test, *Testing Program,* p. 300
- *Alternative Assessment Guide,* pp. 26 and 40
- Suggested Project, *Annotated Teacher's Edition,* p. 255H

Resources
For correlated print and audiovisual materials, see *Annotated Teacher's Edition,* pp. 255A–255B.

STANDARDS FOR FOREIGN LANGUAGE LEARNING
Zum Lesen *Pupil's Edition:* (3.2) *Annotated Teacher's Edition:* (2.2)
Zum Schreiben *Pupil's Edition:* (3.1) *Annotated Teacher's Edition:* (5.1)
Anwendung *Pupil's Edition:* (5.1; 5.2) *Annotated Teacher's Edition:* (1.2)

Komm mit! Level 3

Copyright © by Holt, Rinehart and Winston. All rights reserved.

Teacher's Name _____ Class _____ Date _____

KAPITEL 12 — Die Zukunft liegt in deiner Hand! (Wiederholungskapitel)

Beginning the chapter (pp. 279A–283)

Activities in the shaded boxes enhance the basic lesson and are ideal for **block scheduling**.

Lesson Plans

Chapter Opener

- Do Motivating Activity, p. 279I.
- Have students look at photo #1, p. 280. See the related Teaching Suggestion, p. 279I.
- As students look at photo #1, p. 280, ask your female students if such an occupation would appeal to them. Ask students what is happening to manufacturing jobs in the United States.
- Have students look at photo #2, p. 281. See Thinking Critically: Drawing Inferences, p. 279I.
- As students look at photo #2, p. 281, ask them for information about the concert announced in the poster.
- Have students look at photo #3, p. 281. See the related Teaching Suggestions, p. 279I.
- As students look at photo #3, p. 281, have them answer the question posed in the caption.
- See Focusing on Outcomes, p. 279I.

Los geht's!

Objectives
Students will listen to German teenagers talk about a variety of topics.

- Do Motivating Activity, p. 279J.
- Play the audio recording of **Mitgehört** *(Audio CD 12)* and have students listen with their books closed. Pause after each person speaks and ask students to summarize the teen's remarks.
- Replay the audio recording of **Mitgehört** without pause as students read along in their books.
- For further listening practice, write on the board the names of the speakers and the subjects of their remarks. Then paraphrase the speakers' remarks and have students identify the speakers.
- For further practice with functions, ask students to replace the functional expression(s) that each speaker uses with at least one other synonymous expression. For example, they might have Brigitte say **Ich bin nicht sicher, ...** instead of **Ich weiß noch nicht, ...**
- Have students do Activities 1 and 2, p. 283.
- See Closure, p. 279J.
- Have students do Activities 1 and 2, *Practice and Activity Book*, p. 144.

Resources
For correlated print and audiovisual materials, see *Annotated Teacher's Edition*, pp. 279A–279B.

STANDARDS FOR FOREIGN LANGUAGE LEARNING
Chapter Opener *Pupil's Edition:* (4.1; 4.2) *Annotated Teacher's Edition:* (2.1)
Los geht's! *Pupil's Edition:* (1.2) *Annotated Teacher's Edition:* (2.1)

66 Lesson Planner Komm mit! Level 3

Copyright © by Holt, Rinehart and Winston. All rights reserved.

Teacher's Name _____ Class _____ Date _____

KAPITEL 12 — Die Zukunft liegt in deiner Hand! (Wiederholungskapitel)

Erste Stufe (pp. 284–289)

Activities in the shaded boxes enhance the basic lesson and are ideal for **block scheduling**.

Lesson Plans

Objectives
Students will review reporting on past events, expressing surprise and disappointment, agreeing, giving advice, and giving reasons.

Motivate
- See Teaching Suggestion, p. 279K.

Teach
1. Play the audio recording for Activity 3, p. 284 *(Audio CD 12)*, and check for comprehension.
2. Present **So sagt man das!** and **Ein wenig Grammatik**, p. 284. See Presentation, p. 279K. Have students do Activity 1, *Grammar and Vocabulary Worksheets*, p. 100.
3. Have students write Activity 5, p. 284. See the related Teaching Suggestion, p. 279K.
4. Present **So sagt man das!** *(Expressing surprise and disappointment)*, p. 285. Have students do Activity 1, *Practice and Activity Book*, p. 145.
5. Have students pair off to do Activity 6, p. 285.
6. Have students write Activity 7, p. 285, in class or for homework.
7. Present **So sagt man das!** *(Agreeing; agreeing, with reservations; giving advice)* and **Ein wenig Grammatik** *(The würde-forms)*, p. 285. See Presentation **So sagt man das!**, p. 279K.
8. Play the audio recording for Activity 8, p. 285 *(Audio CD 12)*, and check for comprehension.
9. Have students pair off to do Activity 9, p. 286.
10. Present **Wortschatz,** p. 286. See Presentation, p. 279L. Show *Teaching Transparency 12-1, Teaching Transparencies,* to practice the new vocabulary.
11. Present **So sagt man das!** and **Ein wenig Grammatik**, p. 287. See Presentation, p. 279L.
12. Play the audio recording for Activity 11, p. 287 *(Audio CD 12)*, and check for comprehension. Have students do Communicative Activity 12-1, *Activities for Communication,* pp. 45–46.
13. Have students do Activities 12, 13, and 14, pp. 287, 288. See Group Work, p. 279L.
14. Present **Landeskunde** and have students do Activities A and B, p. 289.

Additional Practice Options for Erste Stufe
- *Grammar and Vocabulary Worksheets*, pp. 100–104
- *Practice and Activity Book*, pp. 145–149
- Communicative Activities 12-1 and 12-2, *Activities for Communication,* pp. 45–46
- Situation 12-1 Interview and Role-playing, *Activities for Communication,* pp. 135–136
- Additional Listening Activities 12-1, 12-2, and 12-3, *Listening Activities,* pp. 95–97 *(Audio CD 12)*
- Realia 12-1, *Activities for Communication,* p. 106
- *Teaching Transparency 12-1, Teaching Transparencies*
- Additional Grammar Practice, *Pupil's Edition,* Activities 1–5, pp. R66–R68

Close
Close, p. 279M

Assess
Quiz 12-1A or 12-1B, *Testing Program,* pp. 257–260, and/or Performance Assessment, p. 279M

Resources
For correlated print and audiovisual materials, see *Annotated Teacher's Edition,* pp. 279A–279B.

STANDARDS FOR FOREIGN LANGUAGE LEARNING

Erste Stufe *Pupil's Edition:* (1.1; 1.3; 2.1; 4.1) *Annotated Teacher's Edition:* (1.3)

Teacher's Name _____ Class _____ Date _____

KAPITEL 12 — Die Zukunft liegt in deiner Hand! (Wiederholungskapitel)

Weiter geht's! (pp. 290–291)

Activities in the shaded boxes enhance the basic lesson and are ideal for **block scheduling**.

Lesson Plans

Weiter geht's!

Objectives
Students will listen to young Germans talk about their plans for the future.

- Do Motivating Activity, p. 279M.
- Before beginning **Pläne für die Zukunft**, have students make a chart of six columns labeled **Studium, Beruf, Heirat, Kinder, materielle Wünsche,** and **nichtmaterielle Wünsche** and numbered from 1 through 5 down the left side.
- Play the audio recording of the first monologue in **Pläne für die Zukunft** (Audio CD 12) as students listen with their books closed. Have students fill in their chart. After checking the content of their chart, ask students how they think this person's plans reflect the modern age.
- Play the audio recording of the second monologue in **Pläne für die Zukunft** and have students fill in their chart. After checking the content of their chart, ask students what this person thinks of Germany. Ask them if they would consider working abroad and why or why not.
- Play the audio recording of the third monologue in **Pläne für die Zukunft.** Have students fill in their chart. After checking the content of their chart, have students compare this person's opinion of Germany with that of person #2. Ask students if they think this girl has a realistic picture of her native land. Is her reason for not living abroad justified?
- Play the audio recording of the fourth monologue in **Pläne für die Zukunft** and ask students to fill in their chart. Check the content of their chart. Ask them what they think of this person's plans.
- Play the audio recording of the fifth monologue in **Pläne für die Zukunft** and have students fill in their chart. After checking the content of their chart, ask them to compare this person's desire for independence with that of person #1. Ask students if they agree with this person that pleasant work is difficult to find in America.
- Replay the audio recording of **Pläne für die Zukunft** in its entirety as students read along in their books. Have them make any additions or corrections to their chart.
- Have students do Activities 15 and 16, p. 291.
- See Closure, p. 279N.
- Have students do Activity 1, *Practice and Activity Book*, p.150.
- Show the video clip **Wohnungsnot der Studenten,** *Video Program (Videocassette 2),* interviews in which several students in Frankfurt talk about their lodgings and the difficulty involved with finding a place to live. See Teaching Suggestions, *Video Guide,* p. 54, and Activity Master 1, *Video Guide,* p. 55.

Resources
For correlated print and audiovisual materials, see *Annotated Teacher's Edition,* pp. 279A–279B.

STANDARDS FOR FOREIGN LANGUAGE LEARNING
Weiter geht's! *Pupil's Edition:* (4.2) *Annotated Teacher's Edition:* (4.2)

Teacher's Name _____ Class _____ Date _____

KAPITEL 12 — Die Zukunft liegt in deiner Hand! (Wiederholungskapitel)

Zweite Stufe (pp. 292–296)

Activities in the shaded boxes enhance the basic lesson and are ideal for **block scheduling**.

Lesson Plans

Objectives
Students will review expressing determination or indecision, talking about what is and is not important, and hypothesizing.

Motivate
See Teaching Suggestion, p. 279N.

Teach
1. Have students read Claudia's letter and do Activity 17, p. 292.
2. Have students write Activity 19, p. 293.
3. Present **So sagt man das!** *(Expressing determination or indecision)*, p. 293.
4. Play the audio recording for Activity 20, p. 293 *(Audio CD 12)*, and check for comprehension.
   Have students do Activities 8 and 9, *Grammar and Vocabulary Worksheets*, p. 105.
5. Present **Wortschatz**, p. 293. See Presentation, p. 279O.
   Have students do Communicative Activity 12-4, *Activities for Communication*, pp. 47–48.
6. Have students pair off to do Activity 21, p. 293.
7. Present **So sagt man das!** *(Talking about what is important or not important)* and **Ein wenig Grammatik** *(Direct and indirect object pronouns)*, p. 294.
   Have students do Activity 4, *Practice and Activity Book*, p. 152.
8. Have students do Activity 22, p. 294.
9. Present **So sagt man das!** *(Hypothesizing)* and **Ein wenig Grammatik** *(Subjunctive forms)*, p. 294. See Presentation, p. 279O.
10. Play the audio recording for Activity 23, p. 294 *(Audio CD 12)*, and check for comprehension.
    Have students do Activities 12–14, *Grammar and Vocabulary Worksheets*, pp. 107–108.
11. Have students work in groups to do Activity 24, p. 295.
12. Have students do Activities 25 and 26, p. 295.
    Have students do Activity 29, p. 296. See the related Teaching Suggestion, p. 279P.

Additional Practice Options for Zweite Stufe
- *Grammar and Vocabulary Worksheets*, pp. 105–108
- *Practice and Activity Book*, pp. 151–154
- Communicative Activities 12-3 and 12-4, *Activities for Communication*, pp. 47–48
- Situation 12-2 Interview and Role-playing, *Activities for Communication*, pp. 135–136
- Additional Listening Activities 12-4, 12-5, and 12-6, *Listening Activities*, pp. 97–98 *(Audio CD 12)*
- Realia 12-2 and 12-3, *Activities for Communication*, pp. 107–108
- *Teaching Transparency 12-2, Teaching Transparencies*
- Additional Grammar Practice, *Pupil's Edition*, Activities 6–10, pp. R68–R69

Close
Close, p. 279P

Assess
Quiz 12-2A or 12-2B, *Testing Program*, pp. 261–264, and/or Performance Assessment, p. 279P

Resources
For correlated print and audiovisual materials, see *Annotated Teacher's Edition*, pp. 279A–279B.

STANDARDS FOR FOREIGN LANGUAGE LEARNING

Zweite Stufe *Pupil's Edition:* (1.1; 1.3; 4.1; 5.1) *Annotated Teacher's Edition:* (3.1; 4.1; 5.2)

Teacher's Name _____ Class _____ Date _____

KAPITEL 12
Die Zukunft liegt in deiner Hand! (Wiederholungskapitel)

Ending the chapter (pp. 297–303)

Activities in the shaded boxes enhance the basic lesson and are ideal for **block scheduling**.

Lesson Plans

Zum Schreiben

Objectives
Students learn to evaluate their writing.

- Do Motivating Activity, p. 279Q, and read and discuss **Schreibtip**, p. 297.
- Have students do Activities A–C, p. 297. See the related suggestions, p. 279Q.

Zum Lesen

Objectives
Students will practice applying reading strategies on their own.

Prereading
- Do Motivating Activity, p. 279R, and read and discuss **Lesetrick**, p. 298.
- Have students do Activities 1–4, pp. 298–299. See the related Teaching Suggestion and Teacher Note, p. 279R.

Reading
- Have students do Activities 5–13, pp. 299–301. See the related Teacher Note, p. 279R, Teaching Suggestion, and Teacher Note, p. 279S.

Postreading
- Have students do Activity 14, p. 301.
- See Closure, p. 279S.
- For additional reading practice, see *Practice and Activity Book*, pp. 155–156.

Ending the chapter

Objectives
Students will assess their achievement of the chapter objectives and review the vocabulary in preparation for the Chapter Test.

- Have students do **Kann ich's wirklich?**, p. 302, individually or with a partner.
- Have students review the vocabulary in **Wortschatz**, p. 303.
- Show **Videoclips: Werbung**, *Video Program (Videocassette 2)*. See Activity Master 2, *Video Guide*, p. 56.

Assessment
- Chapter Test, *Testing Program*, pp. 265–270
- *Test Generator*, Chapter 12
- Speaking Test, *Testing Program*, p. 300
- *Alternative Assessment Guide*, pp. 27 and 41
- Suggested Project, *Annotated Teacher's Edition*, p. 279H

Resources
For correlated print and audiovisual materials, see *Annotated Teacher's Edition*, pp. 279A–279B.

STANDARDS FOR FOREIGN LANGUAGE LEARNING

Zum Lesen *Pupil's Edition:* (3.2) *Annotated Teacher's Edition:* (2.2; 3.2)
Zum Schreiben *Pupil's Edition:* (3.1) *Annotated Teacher's Edition:* (1.1; 1.3)
Ending the Chapter *Pupil's Edition:* (1.1; 1.3; 3.1) *Annotated Teacher's Edition:* (1.3)

Hausaufgaben

Für die Woche von Montag, dem _____ bis Freitag, dem _____

Tag	Aufgaben
Montag, der	
Dienstag, der	
Mittwoch, der	
Donnerstag, der	
Freitag, der	